THE THEORY AND PRACTICE OF
LEARNING

Peter Jarvis • John Holford • Colin Griffin

First published in 1998
Reprinted 1999

Kogan Page Limited
120 Pentonville Road
London
N1 9JN

Stylus Publishing Inc.
2283 Quicksilver Drive
Sterling
VA 20166-2012
USA

British Library Cataloguing in Publication Data

A CIP record for this book is available from the British Library.

ISBN 0 7494 2497 4

Typeset by Kogan Page
Printed and bound in Great Britain by Biddles Ltd, Guildford and King's Lynn

Contents

Preface

Among the most basic of human activities, learning is as crucial as breathing. Learning is the process through which we become the human beings we are, the process by which we internalize the external world and through which we construct our experiences of that world. Without scholars or policy makers appearing to recognize the fundamental significance of this process, learning has assumed a centrality in the educational vocabulary in recent years. Now we talk of the learning organization, the learning society and so on.

Research into human learning has gathered pace over the past century, although much of it is of a more practical than fundamental nature. Even so, recent developments in the practice of helping people learn do not always refer back to some of the earlier research into the learning processes. This book endeavours to rectify this, by introducing readers both to some of the research and to some of the modern practices of learning.

We have written this book for teachers and facilitators, human resource developers, trainers, welfare workers and students of education. It is written in a non-technical language with a limited selection of further reading. But it is not a simple 'how to' book. Instead it aims to provide interested practitioners with a little of the theoretical underpinnings of these modern practices.

The book is divided into three sections: the first two chapters show how and why learning has gradually replaced education in the educational vocabulary; the next five explore some of the more basic theories of learning; and the final seven chapters discuss some contemporary practices and relate them back to the theory.

The three authors were the first members of the Lifelong Learning Research Group in the School of Educational Studies at the University of Surrey. Since its formation in 1996, the group has undertaken a research project, 'Towards the Learning City', subsequently published by the Corporation of London Education Department. The group also organized an international conference on lifelong learning and public policy. A book containing papers developed from this conference will be published by Kogan Page in

1998. The group is currently working on a research project entitled 'Towards an Understanding of Lifelong Learning' in cooperation with educators from the University of Nijmegen in the Netherlands.

This book is a collaboration between members of the group. Each chapter was written by one member and revised after discussion with colleagues. We have decided not to attribute individual chapter authorship. There is one exception to this. The whole of this work was read and criticized by Paul Tosey, who joined the group after this project was started. He also wrote the chapter on the learning organization. We are grateful to him for his invaluable assistance. However, the three main authors must assume responsibility for whatever strengths and weaknesses the book contains.

Peter Jarvis
John Holford
Colin Griffin

The authors

Peter Jarvis is Professor of Continuing Education in the School of Educational Studies, University of Surrey. He is author and editor of many books and papers on education and learning; among his more recent ones are *Ethics and the Education of Adults in a Late Modern Society* (NIACE, 1997) and *The Teacher Practitioner and Mentor in Nursing, Midwifery, Health Visiting and the Social Services* (with Sheila Gibson) (second edition Stanley Thornes, 1997). Later in 1998, Kogan Page will publish a *Human Resource Development Handbook* (which he has written with Pat Hargreaves) and Jossey-Bass will publish *The Practitioner Researcher in the United States*. Peter Jarvis also started and co-edits *The International Journal of Lifelong Education*.

John Holford is Senior Lecturer in the School of Educational Studies, University of Surrey. He moved to Surrey in 1996 after seven years with the University of Hong Kong, and is currently Programme Co-ordinator of the distance learning MSc in Applied Professional Studies in Education and Training. His books include *Reshaping Labour* (Croom Helm, 1988), *Union Education in Britain* (Nottingham University, 1994) and *The Hong Kong Adult Education Handbook* (Longman, 1995; joint author). His current research interests are in the social, cultural and historical aspects of lifelong learning, with particular reference to South East Asia.

Colin Griffin is Associate Lecturer in the School of Educational Studies, University of Surrey, teaching and supervising on the Postgraduate Certificate in the Education of Adults, MSc and PhD programmes. Involved in research projects and publications in the field of curriculum and policy analysis, he has written and translated books and papers in adult education, experiential learning and policy. His published works include: *Curriculum Theory in Adult and Lifelong Education* (Croom Helm, 1983), *Adult Education as Social Policy* (Croom Helm, 1987), *Empowerment through Experiential Learning* (Kogan Page, 1992, joint editor), and 'Policy Science and Policy Analysis' in the *International Encyclopaedia of Adult and Continuing Education* (Elsevier, 1995). His current research interests are in the theory and policy analysis of lifelong learning, with particular reference to critical and postmodern perspectives.

Paul Tosey, the author of chapter 13, is Lecturer in the School of Educational Studies, University of Surrey. He joined the School in 1991, and for five years was responsible for validating and co-ordinating the highly successful MSc in Change Agent Skills and Strategies, an advanced training for organizational development consultants and human resource practitioners. His research and publications are in the field of human processes of change and learning in organizations. He contributed a chapter entitled 'Energies of Organization and Change' to Burgoyne *et al. Towards the Learning Company* (1994). In 1997 he won a University award to pursue research into personal and organizational transformation.

Chapter 1

The emergence of lifelong learning

Like every other social institution, education has undergone many changes over the past few years. The emergence of lifelong learning has been one of them. Significantly, people often now talk about lifelong learning rather than lifelong education, or continuing education, and so on. Understanding these changes and some of the forces that have generated them is important to everyone involved in education and human resource development. So in this first chapter we show what changes have occurred, while chapter 2 provides an introductory analysis illustrating what forces in society have produced these changes.

We shall discuss thirteen shifts that have occurred in society in the last few years. All will be familiar to most providers of learning opportunities. These are not, of course, all the changes which have occurred, and readers may well be able to list others. As we progress through this chapter, we shall also see that there is considerable overlap between them. These thirteen are listed below in the order in which they are going to be discussed. The order does not indicate any causal connotations. The changes are from:

- childhood to adult to lifelong;
- teacher-centred to student-centred;
- face-to-face to distance;
- education to learning;
- the few to the many;
- liberal to vocational;
- theoretical to practical;
- single discipline knowledge to multi-disciplinary knowledge to integrated knowledge;
- knowledge as truth to knowledge as relative;

- rote learning to reflective learning;
- welfare provision (needs) to market demand (wants);
- classical curriculum to romantic curriculum to programme;
- learning as a process to learning as content.

Few of these will come as a surprise to experienced educators, who will be familiar with all of them. Even so, we will discuss each briefly in the remainder of this chapter, which lays the foundations for the remainder of this book.

From childhood to adult to lifelong education

In a strange way education has never really been exclusively a childhood phenomenon, although it has been much more widely recognized in this form. In the United Kingdom, compulsory schooling really only began in 1870, and yet the history of adult education stretches back long before this period (Kelly, 1970). Nevertheless, after 1870, school education grew by virtue of its compulsory nature and education came to be seen by many people as preparing children for adulthood. The history of adult education in the United States reveals many similarities, as Kett (1994) has shown.

Even so, during the twentieth century considerable efforts were made in Britain to emphasize the place of adult education (see, eg, the 1919 Ministry of Reconstruction Report). By the 1960s adult education had become accepted in the United Kingdom, and in that decade there was considerable expansion. The 1944 Education Act had placed various responsibilities on local Education Authorities to ensure the provision of further education within their areas.

Yeaxlee wrote about lifelong education as early as 1929, even though adult education was not then really firmly established in the United Kingdom. But only after the Second World War did signs of adult education's demise as a form of provision appear on the horizon, when UNESCO adopted the idea of lifelong education (Lengrand, 1975). Lifelong education implies that education takes place from birth to death and cannot be limited to certain phases of a person's life.

However, there was not a simple transition from adult education to lifelong education in the United Kingdom. Two other concepts intervened. In the 1960s an idea became popular that people should have an educational entitlement after they left school – this gained ground as recurrent education. Adding to the confusion, the Organisation for Economic Cooperation and Development (OECD) subtitled some of its publications in this period (OECD, 1973) as 'Recurrent Education – a strategy for lifelong education'. The other term that gained popularity was continuing education, that is, education which continued after schooling. This concept carried no implications of educational entitlements and, not surprisingly, it gained ground in the United Kingdom in the 1980s. Continuing education has no end point and so the transition to lifelong education was a simple move which happened in the late 1980s and early 1990s. With the ageing of society, we are now beginning to see an increase in education for the elderly, through the growth of Universities of the Third Age, Elderhostel and other such organizations.

From teacher-centred to student-centred education

In the 1960s some of the more progressive ideas of the American philosopher John Dewey (1916; 1938) were incorporated into school education. Amongst these was his concentration on the child and the way that the child developed. During this period, work by cognitive psychologists, such as Piaget, became quite central to theories about the nature of teaching and learning, and ideas about the developmental stages of growth became central to a great deal of thinking about how children learn.

Significantly, it was during the same period that Malcolm Knowles (1980, *inter alia*), in the USA, popularized his idea of andragogy, which was a student-centred approach to adult education. Some adult educators rightly claimed that this was no new discovery, since adult education had always been student-centred. Be that as it may, Knowles' ideas became extremely popular and his own intellectual pedigree can be traced back to John Dewey through Eduard Lindeman – Knowles' first educational employer and a person who had a great influence on his work. In addition, Knowles' work was published in the 1960s, and was in many ways characteristic of that period.

When the expressive period ended in the mid-1970s, the values of student centred learning had become much more widely recognized, and were often taken for granted in education as a whole. Nevertheless, the extent to which this approach was practised, rather than being merely rhetoric, is open to question.

Nevertheless, the rhetoric of learner-centred education is still very strong, not only in adult education, but also in human resource development, as well as school education.

From face-to-face to distance

Education has traditionally been conducted face to face, with scholars going to where the teacher resides or works. Sometimes this involved peripatetic teachers, or even circulating schools, travelling to wherever the students were. However, it was only in extremely large and sparsely populated countries, like the Australian outback or Russia, that face-to-face tuition could not take place regularly. With the advent of new information technology, all of this was to change.

In 1970, the birth of the British Open University was to be a catalyst in the new information society in education. Liberal adult education courses could be delivered at a distance, through print, radio and television. There was still face-to-face contact, but it played a less significant role. Students could choose the modules they wished to study – and as associate students they did not even have to register for a whole degree course. Modules could be bought off the shelf and studied in the student's own time, in their own place and at their own pace.

The British Open University was a harbinger of things to come, and with the rapid development of information technology, distance education has been transformed yet again. Even the Open University, with its 'Fordist' methods of production (Rumble, 1995) is having to find new markets and new modes of production – and other universities with post-Fordist techniques of production have already been exploiting a global market for education. Education courses are now being delivered electronically and in the United States the electronic university is being pioneered. Other providers are offering opportunities to learn through the World Wide Web, and through other means. Time and space have been transformed in education.

From education to learning

It will be seen throughout this chapter that there has been a gradual move away from the traditional view of education as the means through which the older generation passes on to the next generation the knowledge which it regards as worthwhile and valuable. That previous function of education has now largely disappeared, and education has become more geared to labour market needs – its status has been lowered.

We have also seen different providers emerging in the market who can provide learning materials for potential learners. Education, therefore, is now but one provider among many potential sources of learning material. No longer does it have unique functions highly regarded by society. Now the focus is upon learning – and providers of learning materials no longer have to be educators, or even know about ways of facilitating learning effectively.

Once distance education emerged, traditional teacher-based education was bound to decline, since large teams prepare the learning material but do not have to be present when the learner learns. In addition, learners can and do learn at work. Of course, training, as a concept, carried a much lower status than education, and so the word 'training' has been gently buried – terms like 'human resource development' have emerged and learning is placed at the centre of the process. There has been a deliberate attempt to focus on learning rather than on providers or processes.

From the few to the many

The British system of education was traditionally rather élitist, training the few to assume responsible positions in government, the professions and the Church. Hence, the school curriculum was narrow and selective. A great proportion of children were condemned to non-white collar occupations early in their educational careers. Comprehensive reforms tried to overcome this, but many have doubted whether they succeeded.

By the 1980s, there was still only a small percentage of young people going on to higher education. This was not regarded as a good use of the people's talents and it was certainly not enough to fill all the knowledge-based jobs in society. Reich (1991) implies that about 30 per cent of the United States' workforce should be working in knowledge-based industries. Consequently, the education reforms of the late 1980s and early 1990s in the United Kingdom expanded higher education in the 1990s to a mass system, with more than 30 per cent of young people now able to attend university. This reflects the form of higher education to be found in the United States, but it has not yet arrived in many other countries in the world.

From liberal to vocational

The British Open University began as a 'liberal arts university', since it was easy to offer these courses at a distance. This actually reflected a great deal of the debate which had gone on in school education in the 1960s and early 1970s. Peters (1977), for instance, had argued that the aims of education were to produce a rounded person (an 'educated man') rather than one who was orientated just to work.

However, as education became less welfare-orientated and society developed a more knowledge-based work force (Reich, 1991) so it became more incumbent on people to learn a great deal more about their vocation. Continuing education, which had subsumed adult education, almost became synonymous with continuing professional, or vocational, education. New degree courses mushroomed in universities and colleges of higher education; nearly all were vocationally based.

Employers now became the clients of educational institutions, since it was often they who were paying for their employees' continuing vocational education – the students ceased to be the clients! But employers have specific demands for their own businesses, and educational institutions are much slower to change. Many employers already had large training institutions, which became even more technical and knowledge-based as society changed. Some of these have become much more academically acceptable. Some employers have sought to establish their own universities (Eurich, 1985) – even British Aerospace was reported as establishing its own university in the United Kingdom in 1997. The Labour government has also granted finance for the establishment of a University for Industry.

What has become of liberal education? It has become increasingly categorized as a leisure pursuit. One new trend is toward a new emphasis on third-age education, in the rapidly growing force of non-formal adult educational institutions known in the United Kingdom and elsewhere as Universities of the Third Age.

From theoretical to practical

Until very recently, education in one form or another had a monopoly on teaching all forms of theory. It was generally thought, for instance, that theory had to be taught before new recruits to a profession could go into practice. The idea that practitioners applied theory to practice was widely accepted. It was also widely thought that research was conducted to build up the body of knowledge – it became the theory that could be taught to the next generation of recruits. By the 1970s, this view was being questioned in a number of ways. Stenhouse (1975), for instance, suggested that teachers should research their own practice – after all, they were implementing the curriculum. At the same time, Lyotard (1974) was suggesting that all knowledge in the future would be legitimized through its performability (he later modified the 'all').

Practice became a more central situation in teaching and learning. With the development of experiential learning theories, it is hardly surprising that problem-based education, and then work-based learning, became more significant. Naturally, this was also in accord with industry's own aims to educate its own workforce. Increasingly, for instance, we see continuing education courses, leading to Masters degrees, being totally work-based. Today, we are also beginning to see practitioner doctorates emerge; and with this there is an increasing emphasis on practical knowledge (see Jarvis, 1998).

From single discipline to multi-disciplinary to integrated knowledge

As a result of the Enlightenment and the Industrial Revolution, individual disciplines of study emerged and knowledge about society began be categorized by discipline (philosophy, sociology, psychology, and so forth). Each of the disciplines developed its own array of sub-disciplines, and these sometimes overlapped with each other – social psychology, etc.

By the 1960s, however, this division by disciplines was beginning to be recognized as somewhat artificial, and so ideas of multi-disciplinary study emerged. Consequently, it was possible to study the social sciences and look at each of the social sciences; it was even possible to look at their different interpretations of the same phenomena, so that we could have a philosophy of education, a sociology of education and even a social-philosophy of education. Britain's new universities, especially Keele in the 1960s and the Open University in the 1970s, introduced multi-disciplinary foundation courses. The Open University still retained them as compulsory until the mid-1990s, although pressures to drop multi-disciplinary foundation courses have been quite strong in some quarters.

However, as the orientation to research and study became more practice-based, it was recognized that practice is not multi-disciplinary knowledge but integrated knowledge. Knowledge is now widely recognized to be a 'seamless robe'. Heller (1984) showed how obvious this is for everyday knowledge, and since then the ideas of 'practical knowledge' have emerged. Practical knowledge – such as nursing or teaching knowledge – is integrated and it is knowledge about doing things. It is impossible to divide it into separate elements, since it has never been anything other than an integrated whole. Hence, there is something profoundly different about practical knowledge: it is integrated and subjective. The growth of continuing education vocational courses is to be found in this area of integrated practical knowledge.

From knowledge as truth to knowledge as relative

As early as 1926, the German sociologist, Max Scheler (Stikkers,1980) began to chronicle the way that different types of knowledge change at different speeds, with technological knowledge changing much more rapidly than religious knowledge, etc. Indeed, as early as then he suggested that knowledge seemed to be changing 'hour by hour'. Now technological knowledge is changing minute by minute and second by second. With this rapid change, it is almost impossible to regard knowledge as a truth statement any longer. We are now talking about something that is relative. It can be changed again as soon as some new discovery is made that forces people to change their thinking. The world is awash with new discoveries – this means that there is a greater need for the knowledge-based occupations to keep up with the new developments in knowledge. Hence, we have seen the growth in continuing professional education.

The way that knowledge is changing has been analysed by Lyotard (1984) as narrative. In this way he has tried to retain something of the value-free nature of the concept. Foucault (1972), on the other hand, regarded knowledge as discourse and, for him, discourse is ideological. In this, he recognized that knowledge that becomes public or popular is rarely value-free and, inherently, its perpetuation furthers the cause of certain groups in society rather than others. We could point, for instance, to the way the market has developed and suggest that these changes in knowledge are themselves a function of the market.

From rote learning to learning as reflection

When knowledge was regarded as something true, something that had been verified either by the force of rational logic or by scientific research, then it was to be learnt, that is, to be memorized. Learners were expected to grasp the truth of the scientific discovery and remember it. However, knowledge has become narrative and even discourse. Experts now proclaim in a discourse of technical rationality and it is harder to believe their assertions. We see this especially, for instance, when the expert scientists are called up to address the television cameras that the latest scare will be of no danger to the general public.

Ulrich Beck (1992) has addressed the issue of rapidly changing knowledge by pointing out that society has now become reflexive – that the whole process of change has produced a risk society, and it has become incumbent on society to be reflexive of its own practices. In precisely the same way, learning has changed from remembering 'facts' and 'knowledge' to seeking to understand and be critically aware of the things to be studied. Reflective learning has become much more prevalent because of the processes of change in contemporary society.

From welfare (needs) to market demands (wants)

As a modular approach to the curriculum becomes more acceptable, the idea that education is part of social welfare provision becomes less obtrusive. Now the idea that curricula must meet social needs has become less important, and what the idea of needs means has changed (Jarvis, 1985; Griffin, 1987, *inter alia*). Need no longer refers to a generalized need of potential students, but to various special needs – perhaps those which are residual in society or which can be eradicated through good governance.

Once education ceases to be welfare provision, it can only become market provision. This was precisely what Bacon and Eltis (1976) argued – Britain had to transform its welfare provision into wealth production. This was the economics of monetarism, popularized by the American economist Milton Freidman. Education had to be seen to be a money earner, which was much more simple after the success of the Open University and the realization that its wide choice of modules constituted a market for courses which could be bought 'off the shelf', as it were. Educational needs had turned into a matter of supply and demand – a market.

From classical curriculum to romantic curriculum to programme

The classical curriculum implied that there was only one truth, or proper interpretation, of the material to be taught. This meant there was only one possible way of presenting curriculum knowledge. Such an approach to education was being undermined because it was being recognized that there was more than one possible interpretation of knowledge and, indeed, more than one type of history, religion, and so on, to be taught in a multicultural society. The 1960s saw the development of romantic-type curricula (Lawton, 1973; Griffin, 1983) which explored the opposition between these two approaches.

This pluralistic society led to the recognition that it was becoming increasingly difficult to prescribe precisely what should be taught in the school week, despite many efforts by the government in the 1980s to do just this. By the 1990s, it was generally recognized that these efforts had failed and that there is just too much knowledge to get into every curriculum. Increasingly, optional choices have been built into the system. Now these options have become modules and so education moved to a situation where older children, as well as students in higher education, were presented with programmes of courses from which to choose. The idea of a curriculum is therefore now of limited value. This becomes even more significant as it is realized that the idea that the teachers have the truth to teach is outdated; they can now only act as interpreters of knowledge (Bauman, 1987).

From learning as process to learning as content

The process of learning has generally been understood to be the process through which individuals go in acquiring their knowledge, skills, attitudes, values, beliefs, emotions and senses. Either learning has been regarded as the process of transforming these experiences into human attributes, or – as behaviourists have suggested – learning is seen as the behaviour exhibited as a result of the learning. Both ideas still prevail.

However, more recently, there has been another change in emphasis. The concept of learning places less emphasis on its behaviourist connotations, although it has still retained its product ones. Linguistically, where learning is a process, we are dealing with the verb 'to learn' and learning might be regarded as the present participle. However, when learning is used as a term by itself, as it were, it is the gerund of the verb – that it, the learning is the content of all that has been learnt. Indeed, it matters not whether there was a teacher, or through what process the learning occurred, or even who the provider was – what matters is the learning, and it is valid in itself.

This last meaning is becoming more prevalent in contemporary society.

Conclusion

This chapter has outlined thirteen processes of change that are occurring in contemporary society. We have made no attempt to analyse why they are taking place, since this is the task of the following chapter. Thereafter, we examine some of the major theories of learning and then look at ways in which learning is occurring in contemporary society.

Chapter 2

The social background of lifelong learning

In chapter 1 we outlined some of the main ways in which emphasis is shifting away from education and towards learning. In order to understand how and why this is happening, we have to relate the changes to underlying trends in society itself. This chapter therefore describes the social background to the transition from education to lifelong learning.

Changes in education systems do not take place in a social vacuum. Education has always reflected the forces which shape society. This is true of schools and universities, of course, but also of people's teaching and learning practices as well. Educators can always be tempted to neglect the broader social changes which influence what they do – to reject theory in favour of good professional practice. But good practice does need to be informed by some awareness the world around us. After all, teaching and learning are both social processes.

As we have seen, lifelong learning stands for various new and emerging emphases: learners rather than teachers, programmes rather than curricula, integration rather than specialization, consumer sovereignty rather than institutional provision, and so on. The move from traditional education towards lifelong learning is a prime example of our need to know about the social changes and forces which make this transition so important.

These changes and forces are sometimes very deep. They reflect the balance of power in society, new directions of social and economic policy, and information and communication possibilities opened up by new technology. Changes like this are global in their effects: they are not confined to any one country. Indeed, change has become one of the most universal of human experiences, and the concept of lifelong learning has to be understood in this light. So, before we look at learning, we need to gain some sense of social change in general. This will help us see why lifelong learning has become such a powerful idea in the world, and what it means for education itself.

The focus on change

It is common nowadays to say we live in changing times. This is most obvious in science and technology – information technology in particular. But we cannot really separate technical from social change and the political, economic and cultural changes that accompany it. New technology brings changes in the nature of work, communication, family, community and especially lifestyles. This seems set to continue as far as we can see ahead.

The scale and pace of such changes, according to some social theorists, is so important that they say we are witnessing a new form of society – the 'postmodern'. This is a new stage of human history, with new social, political and cultural forms, and we need new conceptual and theoretical frameworks if we are to understand it. One group of (chiefly French) theorists have been responsible for developing a view of postmodern society. Foucault (1986), Baudrillard (1994), Lyotard (1984) and Bauman (1992), among others, suggest that 'modern' society reflected rationalistic, humanistic and progressive belief systems. But it is being replaced by societies based upon quite different principles. These can only be understood through new concepts and theories of society, the individual and even of thought itself.

But before we look at 'postmodern' society, we need to know what the main features of 'modern' societies were. This is especially important as these were the societies from which traditional education systems emerged. This chapter therefore describes the social origins of education, and then looks at some of the major changes occurring in the world which are bringing about the postmodern conditions which make lifelong learning possible – and even inevitable.

Characteristics of modern societies

The 'modern' period usually refers to the period beginning with the Enlightenment in eighteenth-century Europe, through the Industrial Revolution and the beginnings of the nation state, until nearly the end of the twentieth century.

If the Renaissance stood for the rebirth of classical forms of literature and scholarship after the so-called Dark Ages, the Enlightenment stood for profound social changes connected with science, humanism and individualism. In due course, the kinds of societies we call 'modern' emerged, based upon rationality, freedom and progress. Their main characteristics were as follows.

- The nation state emerged in this period (often quite late) as the universal form of political organization.
- Ideologies of nationalism, community and solidarity arose in various forms – class, status, occupation and so on, usually in some form of hierarchical social structure.
- Ideologies other than nationalism, such as socialism, liberalism, and later Marxism and communism, came to play an important part in social and political life.
- The ideology of progressive humanism played a large part in the struggle for democracy: the belief was that social conditions could be infinitely improved.
- There was a belief in the power of natural science to create material wealth and an ever-increasing degree of control over the environment, as well as in its capacity to improve and extend human life.
- Scientific rationalism came to be applied to controlling social conditions themselves, so that planning and control – in the form of public welfare and education provision – became a typical feature of 'modern' societies.
- The growth of the state was countered by individualism in society. Freedom of conscience and expression became the cornerstones of liberal progressivism and liberal democracy: freedom of the individual was taken to be a logical consequence of belief in science, reason and humanism.
- Science seemed to entail a clear distinction between subject and object, so that objectivity came to be the dominant form of knowledge and way of conducting investigation. This kind of belief made possible the origins of the social sciences themselves.
- Knowledge came to be structured in its own hierarchy, and divided into various separate 'disciplines', which reflected the division between scientific, social, moral and other spheres.
- This kind of division was expressed in the separation of 'high' from 'popular' culture, and in intellectuals' role as the 'keepers' of knowledge on behalf of society as a whole.
- Principles of division and hierarchic structure underlay virtually every aspect of modern society. They could be found in the division of labour in the system of production, and in the bureaucratic organization of modern states.

Needless to say, many of these features of 'modern' societies are still in place. The transition from 'modern' to 'postmodern' continues to be debated in contemporary social theory. Here is how some commentators have defined modernity.

> The dynamics by which modernity produced a new industrial and colonial world can be described as "modernization" – a term denoting those processes of individualization, secularization, industrialization, cultural differentiation, commodification, urbanization, bureaucratization and rationalization which together have constituted the modern world. (Best and Kellner, 1991: 3)

The education systems which arose in modern societies during the nineteenth century have reflected features like these.

Education and modern society

As we have seen, modern societies were characterized by order, stability, a belief in science and progress, shared values and cultural styles, and so on. National education systems developed as a response to the social conditions of industrial society. Nineteenth-century industrial societies applied science and technology to producing the material conditions of life. They were also quite rigidly structured in terms of class and status, and reflected strong beliefs in economic growth and social progress. Everyone 'knew their place'.

Applying science and technology to industry required a skilled workforce to operate machinery. At the same time, industrialization brought rapid social changes. In particular, large urban working classes, and the onset of democratic, humanistic and liberal ideologies called for mass education. This would impart the necessary skills to sustain a modern society, and ensure that each generation was equipped with the values, beliefs and attitudes appropriate to their place in society.

In other words, education has historically functioned as a process of socialization into the established structure and culture of society. Through education everyone got to 'know their place' in a relatively stable and ordered society based on a confident belief in continuity and progress.

Modern education systems originated in societies based on the application of science and technology. They were industrial, commercial and urban societies with mass communications systems, growing populations and increasingly popular political institutions. They reflected beliefs in stability, confidence and progress. To be educated in such a society was therefore to be socialized into it in order to know what to do, what to believe and what to expect.

We may sum up the traditional functions of education thus:

- to transmit the kinds of knowledge and skills required to sustain industrial economies, especially the scientific and technical knowledge on which they were based;
- to reinforce prevailing cultural values in society – the beliefs and attitudes to which people were expected to conform;

- to select the people most fitted to fill the roles which society needed, and to allocate them to an appropriate status or position in society;
- to reconcile people's aspirations with social needs, so that they accepted their place in society.

These mechanisms of education formed part of the process of socialization which was essential – or so it was thought – for society's existence and survival. These functions can still be seen today. Education remains the main vehicle both for allocating social positions and for social mobility. But underlying these mechanisms are some deeper social processes.

- Education maintains and reinforces social order and social cohesion because it encourages people to conform to prevailing norms and culture.
- Education controls and manages individuals' aspirations, so they are 'fitted into' the social structure of employment, class or social status in ways they accept.
- Education therefore reproduces the workforce necessary to an industrial or post-industrial society, with its various divisions of labour, skills, careers and so on.

These are the typical features of education systems as they developed in modern society, and as they have been analysed and theorized by the social sciences.

But of course the social conditions which these educational functions developed from, and to which they were a response, are changing with ever more rapidity. Modern society was a society of stability, certainty and progress: it depended upon shared systems of values, social hierarchies and structures, such as the family, community, and confident expectations for a foreseeable future.

There continue to be elements such as these in our everyday social lives, but the evidence of change is all around us. We need to consider whether the social conditions which produced education continue to be sufficiently strong for it to survive in a recognizable form.

The forces of change

What kinds of development are replacing the old social order of stability, confidence and progress with a world of risk, illusion and ambiguity – and bringing a 'postmodern' society into existence? Even if the postmodern analysis is only partly accurate, the social conditions which education arose from – and within which it functioned – are being replaced. The new conditions call for replacing education with new and different concepts of learning.

This much is already clear in practice. The word 'education' has virtually disappeared from the literature of policy, to be replaced by 'learning'. In this chapter we are seeking to understand why this should happen. Thus, in a whole range of documents and reports, we are beginning to speak of the 'learning society' (EC, 1996; NCIHE, 1997) or of 'lifetime learning' (DfEE, 1996) or of 'lifelong learning' (NIACE, 1997). Learning itself is variously called a 'treasure' (UNESCO, 1996) and a 'joy' (NIACE, 1996). Above all, learning 'works' (FEFC, 1997).

Why have we apparently abandoned 'education' for 'learning' in public and professional discourse? After all, the structures and systems of education – schools, colleges and universities, and so forth – remain in place. The argument here is that although the structure of education remains, the social conditions in which education has traditionally functioned – the conditions we have described as 'modern' – are changing beyond recognition. Among the most important changes are the following.

Globalization

Although the nation state continues to exist, increasingly the world economy is subject to corporate capitalism which knows no national boundaries. As theorists such as Robertson (1992), Giddens (1992) and Hirst (1996) have argued, this is a social and cultural phenomenon, not just an economic one. Globalization has been defined as:

> A social process in which the constraints of geography on social and cultural arrangements recede and in which people become increasingly aware that they are receding. (Waters, 1995: 3)

Demography

The structure of the population is changing. It is ageing. The birth rate is declining. There is more divorce and more people live alone. Over one quarter of all British households consist of just one person. There is less marriage, and people are living longer (Social Trends, 1997). In other words, patterns of family, kinship and domestic life which marked modern society are rapidly breaking down, and the forms of stability and continuity these stood for are being eroded.

Work and the economy

Material goods are no longer mass-produced in industrial factories with large associated workforces, the type of production often now referred to as 'Fordist'. 'Service' industries now form the most important economic sector.

The nature of work itself is changing. The job for life has all but disappeared. The emphasis is on the need for continually developing skills in new technologies. Even the idea of the workplace is changing: in 1995 three in ten male employees in Britain worked from home at some point, and both job turnover and the proportion of the workforce which is economically inactive – not engaged in paid employment – is increasing (Social Trends, 1997).

Privatization

The state's role in many areas of our lives is decreasing as the market in goods and services grows more important. The state is being replaced by forms of 'civil society' which reflect more voluntary and community-based patterns of association. The spreading market economy means that individuals must make their own arrangements for health care, employment, pensions and so on. They can no longer rely on welfare states to provide for them or their families.

Individualization

There is less and less pressure on people to conform to externally imposed values, beliefs or lifestyles. Choice and style are emphasized much more. There are fewer and fewer divisions and distinctions between, for example, high, mass or popular culture. Cultural and value systems are more and more fragmented, as consensus breaks down and individuals become free – and are indeed expected – to take responsibility for their own lifestyles.

Commodification

Individualism and market forces mean that style itself, along with other cultural goods (even knowledge itself), are increasingly seen as commodities. Their value depends on what they can be bought and sold for in the marketplace. Styles of life and culture are replacing traditional systems of value and belief. The media and other forms of communication are replacing production as the basis of social life.

Do all these changes, which are experienced and documented, add up to a form of society so distinct from what went before as to require a total reconceptualization of social life and thought? This is the question of postmodernism. Theorists are still divided on whether we are witnessing a completely new form of society or whether we should regard contemporary developments as a 'late' form of modernity (Giddens, 1993). Some see the moral and cultural relativism of postmodernism as a reactionary and right-wing attack upon the progressive, liberal humanism of the Enlightenment (Habermas, 1992).

Whatever the outcome of such theoretical debates, the issues which arise around postmodernism are of considerable significance. They are now beginning to be explored in the context of education. It is clear that the education systems which developed in modern societies express their values and beliefs.

> Education is very much the dutiful child of the Enlightenment and, as such, tends to uncritically accept a set of assumptions deriving from Enlightenment thought. Indeed, it is possible to see education as the vehicle by which the Enlightenment ideals of critical reason, humanistic individual freedom and benevolent progress are substantiated and realized. (Usher and Edwards, 1994: 24)

Postmodernist thinkers who see education as important in this way point to the failure of education as a source of emancipation for humanity, as well as to recent historical failures of science and humanism in such catastrophes as the Holocaust or Chernobyl (Baudrillard, 1994).

Whether or not we accept this view that education is a failed project of modern society, the new discourse of learning does reflect the changed social conditions we experience today. Education was originally conceived as a process of socialization into a society based upon stability, rationality, objectivity, universality, emancipation and confidence in progress. All of these themes are now under challenge. Education systems traditionally took their place in a system of shared and universal beliefs – scientific, moral, religious or philosophical. They socialized each new generation into a stable and hierarchic society. But once we replace universalism, confidence and progress with risk, illusion and ambiguity, the place of education in the social scheme of things becomes far less clear.

Learning and the postmodern condition

If education seems less appropriate in conditions of postmodernity, why is the focus increasingly on learning? The concluding section of this chapter is concerned with this question. We shall see that there is no single answer. Several social trends and forces are propelling us, inevitably, towards this focus.

There are, first of all, the consequences for our conceptions of knowledge itself. Postmodernists say the 'grand' or 'meta' narratives of knowledge and belief (in science, ideology or religion) are being replaced by a much more fragmentary and relativistic idea of truth. The educational curriculum was based on 'disciplines', or discrete bodies of knowledge, such as history, geography, mathematics and so on. The teacher's role was to be expert in a discipline, explaining it to the student. But now the disciplines are being replaced by more reflexive, pragmatic and experiential approaches, which place the individual learner much more at the heart of the learning process. In post-modern conditions the teacher, intellectual or 'expert', instead of being the 'source' of knowledge, has merely the role of communicator or facilitator (Bauman, 1987). Educators are less and less in a position to determine the curriculum of education. They are cast much more in the role of helping people to learn effectively – in short, they are becoming technicians, rather than authorities.

Second, the content of learning – the 'curriculum' – which used to be determined by the universal structures of knowledge and the authority of the teacher, is being transformed. It has become a mere commodity in a society based on market principles of consumer sovereignty. Postmodern thinkers stress how far society nowadays reflects the supremacy of consumption over production (Baudrillard, 1998; Featherstone, 1990), and of style and symbolism over content and form. One of the distinguishing characteristics of post-modern analysis is its tendency to 'de-differentiation'. This means noticing the erosion between the distinct categories of modernism, such as distinctions between high and popular culture. All such distinctions, once crucial to the discipline structure of education, become arbitrary and subjective. They reflect only individual tastes and styles. In other words, individual learners, rather than 'authorities' and 'experts' – or teachers – are the arbiters of taste and significance.

The importance of learning in the changing way we think and do 'education' is reinforced by other features of postmodern society. Ambivalence has replaced certainty (Bauman, 1991); risk has replaced confidence (Beck, 1992; Lash, 1996). All these theorists think that modern societies rest on the illusion that history progresses along a linear path towards truth and improvement (Baudrillard, 1994). Because postmodernism rejects the possibility of a single progressive path or truth, some socialists and feminists find the whole idea of postmodernism potentially reactionary. As a result, the individual learner has nowhere to turn for disciplined knowledge or certainty – neither science nor belief, philosophy nor ideology, provide a route to truth.

If the social conditions associated with education are stripped away, learning itself must be reconstructed on a much more individualized basis. As in any market, responsibility will rest much more on the individual – the consumer of information. 'Modern' knowledge was rational and universalistic in nature, and this character used to be expressed in the structure and roles of education systems. Now it is being replaced by more reflexive, experiential and pragmatic practices, which have already been partly adopted in the formal education system. The old patterns of certainty, confidence and progress in values, beliefs and authority generally break down, and the individual learner is much more isolated and subject to market forces.

The fate of education is linked with the wider social changes we have discussed in this chapter: changes in culture and lifestyle, work and domestic life, the trends towards the market and civil society and away from state provision, the elements of risk, ambivalence and illusion which are said to characterize postmodern society.

As a consequence of changes such as these, education has been stripped of the socializing function it had in modern society. But this was its *raison d'être*. Postmodern society makes this much more problematic, because the social conditions of socialization have irrevocably changed. In these conditions, the shift from education to lifelong learning (see chapter 1) has to be understood before the new significance of learning theory can be fully appreciated.

Chapter 3

Behaviourist approaches to learning

The behaviourist approach is perhaps the best known of all approaches to learning. It stems from the work of Pavlov and Skinner, although there are other influential behaviourists. It has also been the most common theoretical perspective used in education because it seems functional and scientific. However, we shall examine it in a little more depth and show that it is but one approach to learning and has weaknesses as well as strengths. This Chapter starts by giving a behaviourist definition of learning. Thereafter we examine the work of a number of the best known theorists in this field and analyse their work. The third section discusses conditioning, and finally we turn to teaching and learning.

The problem of definition

Behaviourism emerged after the Enlightenment, as a product of the age of science, when it was generally agreed that the only human data that were scientifically useful were empirical and measurable behaviour. The founder of the behaviourist school was John Watson, who was attracted to earlier thinkers, such as Ivan Pavlov. Of course, we now know that science is more than empirically measurable behaviour, and so today the problems with behaviourism are apparent from the outset. Nevertheless it remains a very popular approach to learning and so it is important to examine it thoroughly.

Borger and Seaborne (1966: 16) provide us with the classic behaviourist definition when they suggest that learning is 'any more or less permanent change in behaviour which is the result of experience'.

From the outset, we notice that the behaviourist definition of learning focuses on the measurable behavioural outcomes of learning, rather than on knowledge, attitudes, values, beliefs and so forth. It is therefore bound to be a very limited approach to learning. Its sole concern is behaviour, but this is not merely observable action. It concerns any form of response to a stimulus that can be measured, although in strict forms of behaviourism only overt responses were considered measurable. More recently, there has been some movement towards more covert forms of behavioural response, although in every case the response has to be measurable.

Why has behaviourism become so well-known an approach in education? It is often assumed that we can measure intelligence and learning by tests and examinations, and that this will give us a clear understanding of what has been learnt. We shall return to this later in the chapter. Now we examine some of the work of the leading theorists of behaviourism who have influenced education and learning.

Behavioural theorists

In this section, we shall look briefly at five of the theorists most frequently cited in the behaviourist literature on learning: Pavlov, Thorndike, Watson, Skinner and Hull.

Ivan Pavlov

In most people's minds, Pavlov is associated with his work with dogs, although he actually won the Nobel Prize in 1904 for his work on the physiology of digestion. His research showed that dogs salivated at the sight of dry food. If a buzzer sounded just before the dogs were given sight of the dry food they still salivated at the sight of the food. After the two were associated in this way a number of times, the dogs salivated at the sound of the buzzer, even before the food appeared. Therefore, it can be claimed that the dogs had learnt to salivate at the sound of the buzzer.

Pavlov called the presentation of the food the unconditioned stimulus and the salivation the unconditioned response. He regarded the association of the food with the buzzer as the conditioned stimulus. The salivation prior to appearance of the food he termed the conditioned response. This, then, is the basis of classical conditioning.

Although Pavlov did not make any other claims for his experiments than this, other behaviourists have used his work as the basis for more extensive claims about learning.

Edward L Thorndike

At much the same time as Pavlov's work in Russia (the end of the nineteenth century) Thorndike was doing similar work in America. His work was with cats and food. He put a cat into a cat box which had a lever to open the door, and placed food just beyond the cat's reach, though it could see the food through the bars. As the cat struggled to reach the food, it eventually pressed the lever and the door opened. When the experiment was repeated, Thorndike discovered that the cat gradually learnt to associate the lever with opening the box, so that it got to the food more quickly. Hence Thorndike proposed a law of effect which specified that responses to a situation which are followed by satisfaction will be strengthened, and responses that are followed by discomfort will be weakened. In his later work, Thorndike tended to emphasize the first part of this law and to play down the significance of the latter part.

In Thorndike's work we see early experiments with the types of trial-and-error learning that goes on in everyday life, especially when we are seeking to solve problems. Thorndike, however, did not locate his work within this context.

John B Watson

Watson was the person who first used the term 'behaviourism'. His position was more extreme than many, since he actually denied the existence of the mind. Cognitive experiences to him were merely epiphenomena to behaviour. Watson was influenced by Pavlov, among others, and extended this work to human learning along lines similar to Thorndike. He proposed two laws relevant to our concerns – the law of frequency and the law of recency. The former suggests that, the more frequently a stimulus and a response are associated, the stronger the habit will become. The second asserts that the response that occurs most recently after a stimulus is most likely to be associated with it.

B Frederic Skinner

Like his predecessors, Skinner worked with animals and food. He found that rats would learn to push down a lever in order to get food. He used a similar box with pigeons. Consequently, he formulated two laws: that of conditioning and that of extinction. The former specifies that a response followed by a reinforcing stimulus is strengthened and is more likely to occur again. The latter states the opposite. Skinner is regarded as the founder of operant conditioning, as opposed to the classical conditioning formulated by Pavlov.

Unlike Watson, however, Skinner recognized that mind plays a significant role in human learning.

Clark L Hull

Hull's work was influential in behaviourism for a number of years, since he proposed that there are intervening variables in the stimulus-response equation, such as the strength of the habit to be broken and the strength of the internal drive that motivates the behaviour.

With few exceptions, behaviourism was based on research which concentrated on stimulus and response in animals. Although little of the research examined human learning, the results of the research are often said to apply to human beings. The logic on which this transfer from animals to humans is made is dubious. For instance, Watson claimed that cognitive processes were mere epiphenomena to behaviour, but this is difficult to accept if we consider mathematical or philosophical reasoning. It is also difficult to accept that the human race is deluded into thinking that its thought processes are more significant than epiphenomena. At the same time, this school of thought has been very influential in human learning theory.

Conditioning

Two forms of conditioning emerge from this research: classical conditioning, associated with Pavlov, and operant conditioning, associated with Skinner.

Classical conditioning

This is the process where an unconditioned response (salivation) is elicited not from the unconditioned stimulus (food) but from a conditioned stimulus (sound of the buzzer). When the response is elicited only from the conditioned stimulus, it is regarded as a conditioned response. The learning associated with this process is the association of the conditioned stimulus with the unconditioned stimulus and the production of the same outcome. Clearly this approach works with human beings just as much as it does with animals. For instance, students might learn to like a subject because they unconsciously associate it with a teacher whom they like or a pleasant atmosphere in the classroom.

It might be argued that this form of conditioning is not really learning, as it is merely reflexive. However, some psychologists are now beginning to suggest that there is actually a cognitive dimension to the process, since the association is not really between the stimuli (conditioned and unconditioned) but between the mental representations of the stimuli, and that this might enable individuals to predict outcomes (see Ormrod, 1995: 39).

Operant conditioning

In this form of conditioning, the conditioned response is reinforced by a succeeding stimulus – perhaps the response is brought under stimulus control. In a sense, it could be claimed that the stimulus takes control of the response and that the outcome is, thereafter, predetermined. Some psychologists make a distinction between operant conditioning and instrumental conditioning. The former allows for 'free' or discovered conditioned response, whereas instrumental conditioning specifies that the subject must perform the specified acts within the trial situation. This is really only a special case of operant conditioning, but we will look at it again below.

There are many forms of reinforcer, both positive and negative. The former might be used to induce the types of response that are required and the latter to prevent unwanted responses occurring. Parents and teachers are aware of the usefulness of reinforcers of both forms. Praise is a positive reinforcer while punishment is a negative one.

Teaching and learning

From the above discussion two diametrically opposing approaches to teaching and learning emerge. One gives a great deal of freedom to the learner, while the other takes away whatever freedom the learner has. Here, in a sense, we see the difference between operant conditioning and instrumental conditioning.

Trial-and-error learning

This approach to teaching and learning might also be called 'discovery learning' or 'problem solving'. This occurs in many walks of life. We learn by trial and error during everyday life; for example, when we enter a new situation and seek to find out how we are expected to behave. We can do the same in educational situations. Problem solving has become one of the major concerns in contemporary society and the teaching of problem solving has become a significant concern for many educators.

Teachers and lecturers can allow students considerable freedom to undertake projects and experiments and discover for themselves the outcomes of their work. Much problem-based learning focuses on trial-and-error-type approaches to learning situations. When trial and error is a project without a great deal of teacher intervention, then the only conditioning that occurs is that which occurs as a result of learning in the process. Students are conditioned by the positive outcomes – pleasure or satisfaction – of their experience.

However, teacher intervention can change this situation by providing positive reinforcement when the trials are going right and negative reinforcement when the outcomes are incorrect. When they do this, teachers are also using a form of operant conditioning. The degree of teacher intervention is clearly a matter for the teacher to decide. If there is a great deal, the element of trial or discovery is removed and the direction of the learning process and its outcome is controlled by the teacher.

Instrumental teaching

Amongst the most common forms of learning found today in schools and colleges is that where the learning outcomes are specified in behavioural terms. Behavioural objectives are expected to be specified by many schools, colleges and examining boards. Teachers and lecturers are expected to write their lesson plans in terms of:

- 'At the end of the lesson, students will be able to do…'
- 'At the end of the lesson, students will know…'
- 'At the end of the lesson, students will have the skills to…'

The point about these objectives is that they are behavioural outcomes that can be measured. Speaking, writing and doing are all behavioural outcomes. So long as the learning can be measured, it is behavioural, even if what is learnt is cognitive – since, as we have seen, some behaviourists do not accept that there is a mind.

These are common formulations about how the teacher's role is perceived. Clearly there is nothing wrong with having a high degree of precision, but when the conditioning takes away the learner's freedom, the system and the teacher's role need to be considered carefully. Indeed, the morality of such practices needs to be thoroughly considered. What right has the system, or the teacher, to take away the student's autonomy? (See Peters, 1966; Jarvis, 1997 for further discussion on this topic.)

This approach to teaching can also be seen as indoctrination, since the teacher is seeking to control the student's learning in order to produce the desired results. The teacher can be expected to use whatever positive or negative reinforcers are necessary to ensure that 'correct' outcomes are achieved.

However, it is not only the morality that is problematic. This approach produces outcomes which are conformist and, to some extent, reliant upon those in authority who specify what form of behaviour is 'correct'. In this sense, the learning is reproductive, and it makes education open to all the criticisms of scholars in the past to its being socially and culturally a state, or a company, system of reproduction (Bourdieu and Passeron, 1977). It might also be claimed that in the long run this approach to learning is not very efficient, because it has not encouraged the learners to think for themselves, but only to learn to conform to the accepted position.

Obviously, this approach is applicable to therapy and behaviour modification, especially aversion therapy. Indeed, therapy is the utilization of such techniques in order to try to get children or adults to perform certain types of behaviour and not others. Therapy, of course, is not education, but it does involve learning.

What then of skills learning – is this not behavioural? Of course it is, but learning a skill does not have to be undertaken in the same way as the military services used to drill new recruits by 'square-bashing' to produce conformist servicemen and servicewomen. Skills can be taught by much more open methods, such as trial and error, which do not take away the learner's freedom, although correct behaviours can still be positively reinforced.

Conclusion

Behaviourist-type approaches have also underlain much of the rather sterile debate about the differences between education and training. We do not find this distinction helpful. There is much to commend in trial-and-error-type behavioural approaches, and behavioural/skills learning of this kind is not only educational, it is very important both in the world of work and the world of leisure.

We live in an instrumentally rational age in which the end-product has always been more important than the means. Teachers are expected to get immediate and measurable results, and schools and colleges have to do the same. We have seen the emergence of competency-based education in the past decade or so, and an increasing emphasis on National Vocational Qualifications which seek to assess levels of competency. While measurable outcomes are not the only reason for this development, they certainly make a contribution.

We can see from the above that behaviourism is an instrumental approach to teaching and learning. When it comes to human beings, instrumentalism is of dubious value and morality. Why then is it widely accepted and practised? It gets results. The ends justify the means! This is a maxim which is frequently heard in our society – but there are questions to be answered. Does it really get results? Are short-term ends always the best ones? Logic would suggest that this is not the case, although common sense would find this hard to accept.

Finally, we should add that few of the early behaviourists thought that they had understood the whole of the learning process. They recognized that their research was a small part of understanding the human being – it was only with Watson that inclusive claims for behaviourism were made, and these were accepted by Skinner. Human beings are more complex than just the sum of their behaviours. Education for a considerable period of time seemed to play down behaviour in order to emphasize cognition – the very thing that Watson rejected.

The following chapters of this book explore other theories of learning which start from different perspectives and even have different definitions of learning!

Chapter 4

Cognitivist theories

After the behaviourist theories came cognitive ones. The leading and most influential cognitive theorist in the West was Piaget, although Vygotsky's work has been much more influential in Eastern Europe. We might have left Vygotsky until the next chapter, as his approach is also interactionist and similar in many ways to George Herbert Mead's. Piaget and Vygotsky both offer developmental theories. The one writer we look at in this chapter who writes from a specifically adult education background, Jack Mezirow, has almost no developmental element to his work.

The chapter, therefore, falls into three parts. The first examines the work of Piaget and those whose theories have followed directly from his work; the second examines Vygotsky's work; while the final section looks at Mezirow's theory of transformative learning.

Jean Piaget

Piaget (1929, *inter alia*) wrote in the first half of this century. He concentrated on in-depth studies with small samples of children, including his own daughter. This was both a strength and a weakness. The work is in-depth, but the weakness lies in the fact that case studies and small samples cannot be legitimately generalized. Nevertheless, his work has been tremendously influential in school education for many years, because he outlined the way children developed cognitively in a series of books. For him, learning related to the stage of children's cognitive development. The closer the content to be learnt matched the level of cognitive development, the better.

Piaget's is a stage theory and can be summarized in the following table, taken from a summary overview of his work (Jarvis, 1972).

Table 4.1 *Piaget's stages of cognitive development*

Period	Age (in years)	Characteristics
Sensori-motor	0–2	Infant learns to differentiate between self and objects in the external world
Pre-operational thought	2–4	Child ego-centric but classifies objects by single salient features
Intuitive	4–7	Child thinks in classificatory way but may be unaware of classifications
Concrete operations	7–11	Child able to use logical operations such as reversibility, classification and serialization
Formal operations	11–15	Trial steps towards abstract conceptualization occur

As can be seen from Table 4.1, Piaget's concerns focused upon the fact that as children grow older, so their ability to conceptualize develops.

Apart from the initial criticism we made of Piaget's work, there are at least two others. First, his analysis stops at the age of fifteen, whereas individuals continue to grow and develop cognitively. Although he did not continue his studies in this way, Piaget recognized that thought patterns continue to develop. One of the clearest summaries of what occurred in research about adult development following Piaget's approach is to be found in Allman's work (1984: 75). She wrote:

> The results of [Arlin's 1975] study revealed that the ability to ask or discover important questions develops subsequent to the stage of formal operation which results in deriving answers to questions and solutions to problems. Neugarten's (1977) research into middle-aged people's thinking strategies identified an increasing use of reflective thinking. Whereas Moshman's (1979) suggested... the ability to think about one's own theories and processes of theorizing also develops subsequent to formal operational thought.

Allman continues with a discussion of Riegel (1973) whose work also points us beyond the formal operational thought mode. He recognized that adults think in dialectical operational terms. This, Allman (1984: 76) describes as:

> ... a type of thinking which results in the discovery of important questions and problems. This demands the abilities to tolerate contradictions and to use the tension between the two or more contradictory explanations as a creative force which allows for the discovery of new questions and problems.

Thus the main foci of developmental cognitive theorists after Piaget have been upon reflection and dialectic thought. Both have become central to our thinking about adult learning in recent years.

The second criticism of Piaget is that, for him, the stages of cognitive development are relatively discrete. Bruner (1968: 27), for instance, claimed that:

> mental growth is not a gradual accretion... It appears more like a staircase with rather sharp rises, more a matter of spurts and rests. The spurts ahead seem to be touched off when certain capacities begin to be developed. And some capacities must be matured and nurtured before others can be called into being.

Both Kohlberg and Fowler have, however, produced stage theories which are neither so discrete nor so specifically age-related. Both have become leading theorists in their own fields of moral development and faith development respectively. Although neither morality nor religious faith is central to this book, Kohlberg and Fowler are both cognitive, developmental learning theorists. We therefore briefly summarize their work as we bring this section to a close.

Lawrence Kohlberg

Kohlberg regarded Piaget's stage theory as too simple, and discovered that individuals mix their modes of thought in moral development. Kohlberg (1986: 34–5) proposed six stages of moral development without reference to age, as Table 4.2 (summarized from Jarvis, 1997: 57) illustrates.

Thus Kohlberg's work, which has become very influential, builds on Piaget's but shows that people's cognitive moral development is not entirely age-related. He discovered that, at any one time, people's conceptual level contains a mixture of different stages of development. Indeed, according to Kohlberg, many people do not achieve the higher levels of morality at all.

Table 4.2 *Kohlberg's model of moral development (summarized from Jarvis, 1997: 57)*

Level 1 –	**Pre-conventional**	
Stage 1 –	Heteronomous morality	– sticks to the rule
Stage 2 –	Individualism /instrumentalism	– concrete individual interest, aware of other people's interests
Level 2 –	**Conventional**	
Stage 3 –	Mutual interpersonal expectations	– lives up to others' expectations in order to be seen to be good and can then have self-regard as good
Stage 4 –	Social system and conscience	– fulfils social duties in order to keep the social system going
Level 3 –	**Post-conventional**	
Stage 5 –	Social contract	– upholds relative rules in the interest of impartiality, welfare for all
Stage 6 –	Universal ethical principles	– follows self-chosen ethical principles, even when they conflict with laws

James Fowler

Fowler (1981) was influenced by both Piaget and Kohlberg and devised a similar stage theory for religious faith development. Once more there are six stages, although Fowler also adds a pre-stage which he calls infancy. He suggests ages for the earlier stages, but again not everybody reaches the higher levels of development. In order to show the similarity among these developmental approaches, we have summarized Fowler's theory in Table 4.3.

Both Kohlberg and Fowler extend Piaget's ideas without moving a great deal beyond the cognitive. They were also influenced by Erikson (1965) and by studies such as Levinson's (1978) *Seasons of a Man's Life*. For our purpose, they all demonstrate how cognitive psychology has influenced our ideas about human learning.

Table 4.3 *Fowler's stages in faith development*

Stage 1 – Intuitive-Projective	– Egocentric, becoming aware of temporality, productive of image formation that will affect later life
Stage 2 – Mythical-Literal	– Aware of the stories and beliefs of the local community which begins to provide coherence for experience
Stage 3 – Synthetic-Conventional	– faith extends beyond family, provides a basis for identity and values
Stage 4 – Individual-Reflective	– self-identity and world outlook are differentiated, explicit system of meaning develops
Stage 5 – Conjunctive	– Faces the paradoxes of experience, begins to develop universals and becomes more other-orientated
Stage 6 – Universalizing	– Rarely achieved, totally altruistic and their felt sense of the environment is inclusive of all being

Significantly, it is possible to argue that a great deal of human development is not age-based but experiential. When we look at experiential learning theories, we shall see that people deal with situations and construct new experiences based upon their past experiences, both conscious and unconscious. Before we do this, however, we must examine the work of Vygotsky.

Lev Vygotsky

Apart from some Finnish scholars (eg Engestrom, 1987; 1990), Vygotsky's work has been less widely known and less influential in the West than

Piaget's (until recently: see, eg Dovey, 1997a). Vygotsky knew Piaget's work and, like him, undertook his research with children, but he had a consciously different orientation from earlier cognitive theorists. In Piaget's work, for instance, cognitive development seems to precede the learning. Development is a substitute for innate reflexive responses, and only when a certain level of development has been reached is it possible to comprehend a concept. Vygotsky (1978: 85), on the other hand, wanted to discover 'the actual relations of the developmental process to learning capabilities'. In order to do this it was necessary to determine two different developmental levels: the actual developmental level and the zone of proximal development.

The actual developmental level is the level of the child's mental functions as a result of developmental cycles which have already been completed. For Vygotsky, mental age equated to the actual level of development. However, he thought that what children do with the assistance of others might be an even better indication of their mental development than what they achieve by themselves. This led him to posit a zone of proximal development (1978: 86). This he defined as:

> the distance between the actual developmental level as determined by independent problem solving and the level of potential development as determined through problem solving under adult guidance or in collaboration with more capable peers.

Here Vygotsky points to potential rather than achievement. But he also points out the value of collaboration rather than total independence when trying to assess achievement levels or intelligence. Potential is a much more dynamic concept than achievement. This means that imitation is a significant element in learning. We can only imitate what is within our developmental level; we cannot imitate those things that lie beyond our zone of proximal development at any time. From this Vygotsky (1978: 88) concluded that 'human learning presupposes a specific social nature and a process by which children grow into the intellectual life of those around them'. Children, therefore, need support systems (scaffolding) in order to undertake tasks within the zone of proximal development. Based on this, Vygotsky (1978:90) reached a most significant conclusion:

> ... developmental processes do not coincide with learning processes. Rather, the developmental process lags behind the learning process; this sequence then results in zones of proximal development.

The importance of this for learning theory is that we cannot draw inferences from what individuals do independently. We need to try to see their potential rather than their achievements. He suggested that potential can be spotted in teamwork and through guidance and coaching. Indeed, Vygotsky is clear that different individuals have different-sized zones of proximal development and, consequently, different potential within that specific context.

In another area of his work Vygotsky points to a further significant feature about human learning; this is in the realm of meaning. In 'a dynamic system of meaning... the affective and the intellectual unite,' he suggests (Vygotsky, 1986: 10). However, the affective has been absent from much analysis of meaning in Western thought, although Boud *et al.* (1985) rightly included the affective in their analyses of experiential learning and, more recently, Goleman (1995: 284) has argued that emotional literacy improves children's academic achievement. Once more Vygotsky returned to Piaget, but then proceeded to develop his own theoretical orientation to the development of verbal thought. In carefully controlled studies he traced the relationship between motive, inner speech, meanings and external speech. He did not claim that the relationship was unchanging or that he fully understood it, but he concluded (1986: 253) that:

> To understand another's speech, it is not sufficient to understand his words – we must understand his thought. But even that is not enough – we must know its motivation.

Indeed, Vygotsky believed that only when we have reached this level can we really understand the communicative process. Perhaps we in the West have omitted the emotional element in meaning and in learning to our detriment.

Jack Mezirow

The final theorist whose work we are going to examine in this chapter is Jack Mezirow, an American adult educator. His work is less concerned with development, although he does (1991: 7) define adult development as 'an adult's progressively enhanced capacity to validate prior learning through reflective discourse and to act upon the resulting insights'. However, his main focus is on meaning and the transformation of meaning perspectives. This is a much more cognitive approach than Vygotsky's analysis of meaning (Mezirow does not appear to know Vygotsky's work). Mezirow recognizes that feelings play a part in this process, but they receive little emphasis in his work.

Mezirow (1990: 2) differentiates between meaning schemes and meaning perspectives. Meaning schemes are symbolic models (such as images) which we project upon sense impressions of the world in order to construe meaning and habitual expectations. Habitual expectations govern if–then, cause and effect, category relationships, and event sequences, such as turning a knob and expecting a door to open. They are the implicit rules for interpreting our experiences. Meaning perspectives, however, are higher-order theories, beliefs and propositions. The distinction between the two is sometimes very unclear in Mezirow's work. However, we do not enter a critical debate with him here, since our concern is with cognitive learning theories and his emphasis on meaning.

Meaning is always an interpretation of experience based upon our previous experiences, our meaning systems and the language we use. However, there is a danger in this: we can impose our meaning systems on our present experience in an uncritical manner, rather than seeing things as they 'really are' (Mezirow, 1991: 5). For Mezirow, what we have to do is be critical of this process.

Indeed, Mezirow's concern seems to be that transformative learning involves the process of self-reflection upon these meaning perspectives, which 'may result in the elaboration, creation, or transformation of meaning schemes' (Mezirow, 1991: 6). This is at the heart of Mezirow's theory. Transformative learning results in meaning schemes being transformed, new schemes created and different perspectives gained on experience itself.

Strongly influenced by Habermas, Mezirow is also concerned about instrumental and communicative learning. Instrumental learning involves 'cause–effect relationships and learning through task-orientated problem solving' (Mezirow, 1991: 73). Communicative learning, on the other hand, necessitates 'the learner actively and purposely negotiat(ing) his or her way through a series of specific encounters by using language and gesture and by anticipating the actions of others' (Mezirow, 1991: 78). The former is about prescription, whereas the latter is about 'insight and attaining common ground through symbolic interaction' with other persons. For Mezirow, this is not a dichotomy but two distinct types of learning. Both are utilized in many human activities.

Mezirow's theory, as a theory of learning, is limited in certain ways. Its major concern is with the meaning schemes and perspectives, rather than with the actual processes of adult learning. At the same time, it provides a significant emphasis on how we construe our experiences and the significance of the meaning schemes we impose upon them. As we develop as adult human beings, these are transformed. Although we have pointed to a major limitation of Mezirow's approach as a theory of learning, the extensive recent debate about the validity of his formulation lies beyond the scope of this book.

Conclusion

These cognitive theories are all concerned in a variety of ways with human development. While Piaget's rather crude stage theories have been surpassed by recent theorists, the more experientially based approaches seem to provide a better understanding than the age-related theories. Only with Vygotsky's zone of proximal development does the potential to grow and develop occupy a significant place in learning theory. Only with Vygotsky too is the affective domain regarded as a central part of the cognitive.

Chapter 5

Social learning

Learning has often been studied through examining how individuals learn. But learning clearly has a social dimension or context. We learn from and alongside other people, in all our social relationships. This is particularly evident in education, which involves relations between teachers and learners, and between learners themselves. Much of what has been described as schooling's 'hidden curriculum', for instance, consists of what children learn by their social relationships, rather than as a result of what they are 'formally' taught. For adult learners too, supportive social relations, whether in the classroom, family or workplace, are known to be significant factors in the motivation to learn.

There is another way of thinking about the social context of learning. This lies in the social purposes for which people learn. These may be collective: to advance the interests of a particular group, such as an excluded social minority, or a community; or to raise the level of awareness and consciousness of a particular section of society. In fact, education to achieve social ends is as old as education itself. Education, after all, begins with the need for literacy, employment skills, citizenship or simply the capacity for effective participation in society.

All these threads have been gathered together in lifelong learning, which brings the social nature of learning very much to the fore. Policies for lifelong learning make frequent reference to the 'learning society', the 'learning culture', and the need to establish the family, the community and the workplace as foci of learning (NAGCELL, 1997). The concept of the 'learning organization' is well-established (see chapter 13).

But how can groups or collectivities be said to learn? If they do, is the process analogous to that of the ways in which individuals themselves learn, or does it have its own distinctive features and character? Is group learning any more than the sum total of the learning of the individuals who comprise the group?

There are in fact many different ways in which learning can be said to be social. This chapter can only deal with some of the most important. Contributions from sociology, psychology and social psychology have focused on different issues. From a sociological perspective, individuals are socialized into cultural values, attitudes and beliefs. They come to share these with the rest of society, which makes possible the consensus on which all societies are said to depend for their survival. From a social psychological perspective, the individual 'self' is a social construct, and individual learning is a function of social relations. For psychologists, learning may be seen as a process of interaction between individuals and their social environment. In this chapter we outline these positions, and then assess their relevance for education and lifelong learning. We try to show that these differing perspectives on social learning are not mutually exclusive. Each offers an insight into how all learning has some social dimension. We shall look particularly at the work of Jarvis (1987), Mead (1934) and Bandura (1977).

Learning, culture and social roles

All human learning takes place in a social or cultural context. Sociology has contributed to our understanding of learning through the concept of socialization. This refers to the process by which individuals internalize the values, beliefs and norms of behaviour of the society into which they are born. Early sociologists (Durkheim, 1964; Parsons, 1951; Merton, 1968) in fact provide us with a model of social learning. They viewed human society as a sort of living organism, rather like the human body itself. In order to maintain, survive and reproduce itself, society had to adapt to its changing environment. Societies and individuals which did not adapt, they argued, did not survive. This particular sociological perspective, called functionalism, has long been abandoned, but lifelong learning policies still exhort us to learn to adapt to survive. More recent sociological perspectives, such as social interaction theory, also provide insights into social learning.

Later in this chapter we shall also consider perspectives from social psychology. This also looks at learning in the context of our interaction with other individuals in society. The theme of learning as interaction with the social environment is also involved in the concept of the 'learning organization', which we discuss in chapter 13.

Thinking of society as a kind of living organism has certain implications. In particular, it leads to the view that individual societies require certain functions to be performed if they are to adapt and survive. This is why the perspective is called functionalism. One of the most important of such functions was socialization, which is simply the name for how individuals learn to be members of society. This perspective has been criticized as conservative, and for its monolithic view of society. Critics argued that functionalism implied that all individuals were simply moulded to accept the prevailing status quo. Society, they said, does not just reflect universal shared values. Important class, gender and ethnic divisions exist. Nevertheless, the functionalist way of thinking continues to be reflected in everyday or 'common sense' beliefs about change, adaptation, evolution and survival.

Sociological functionalism represents an important model of social learning. It draws attention to how social learning occurs in several ways.

- Societies have to learn functional adaptation in order to survive in a changing environment.
- Individuals must learn social roles in order to be members of society.
- Failure to learn means that society itself will not survive, and that individuals will come to play deviant or dysfunctional roles.

In particular, the idea that learning consists of social adaptation by individuals has continued to be a very powerful one. It is reflected in psychological and educational thought, as will be seen, and continues to be seen as relevant to how people learn.

In his work on the social context of adult learning, Jarvis stressed the significance of cultures and sub-cultures for our understanding. He adopted a sociological perspective on learning:

> ... the position adopted here is that learning is not just a psychological process that happens in splendid isolation from the world in which the learner lives, but that it is intimately related to that world and affected by it... Hence, it is as important to examine the social dimension of adult learning as it is to understand the psychological mechanisms of the learning process. (Jarvis, 1987: 11–12)

Jarvis argues that the culture of society is 'objectified' for the individual through the socialization process, schooling and so on. In this way, individuals acquire or 'internalize' the knowledge, values, beliefs and attitudes of society. This is not a process exclusively associated with childhood. It continues throughout life, through what sociologists call 'secondary socialization'.

Sociologists of education have given a lot of attention to social learning in the form of socialization. They have developed many theories of the curriculum – in schools and post-compulsory education – along these lines. Jarvis cites Bernstein (1971) and Lawton (1973). Their studies of social class, linguistic codes and the construction of the curriculum reflect a sociological view of educational processes and a concept of social learning.

Jarvis reflects the common criticism of sociological functionalism. He sees it as presenting a view of individuals as merely passive and conformist recipients of the prevailing cultural values of society. The relation between individual and society is more complex, he suggests. It should be understood as involving interaction and mutual influence:

> All aspects of the individual are, to some degree, a reflection of the social structure. But this is not merely an acquisition, or receptive process, since this social self affects the manner in which persons perceive and interpret their experiences in social living... individuals actually modify what is received and it is the changed version that is subsequently transmitted to other people in social interaction. (Jarvis, 1987: 14)

Jarvis therefore presents a social theory of learning in this sense. The idea of a social self means that all our learning takes place in an interaction between ourselves and others, and in the context of prevailing beliefs and attitudes – what we call the culture of society. This is not a one-way transaction, but it does make socialization a primary function of learning.

From this sociological perspective, therefore, the structure and culture of society determine how any individual learning can take place. It criticizes behavioural approaches to learning by stressing that human learning is self-conscious and reflexive. We are both products and creators of culture. Learning is seen not as social adaptation but as social action and interaction. What is clear, from this perspective at least, is that learning can only be conceived as a social activity. It is important to remember, however, that this remains a view of how individuals learn. This particular sociological perspective does not imply that social groups, or society itself, can be said to learn. We can take this view if we also see society as a kind of living organism which must learn in order to survive and reproduce itself. This view, to which we shall return, corresponds to the theory of social evolution.

In the meantime, we must examine a perspective from social psychology. This will enable us to develop the concept of the social self further, and to explore its significance for the theory of learning.

Mead and the social construction of self

George Herbert Mead (1863–1931) was one of the most influential social psychologists. He took the idea of the social context of learning well beyond the concepts of individual adaptation and interaction. The very concepts of self and mind, he believed, could only be explained as social processes. Like functionalism in sociology, Mead's theory owes much to Darwin's view of evolution and to the philosophy of pragmatism. Influenced by Darwin, Mead saw the self and the mind as emerging from the natural processes of adaptation and adjustment to the environment, rather than as spiritual or metaphysical entities. He argued that evidence for the mind or the self could only be derived from how they manifest themselves socially.

Mead's chief work, *Mind, Self and Society* is subtitled *From the Standpoint of a Social Behaviourist*. This approach presupposes some kind of social structure, or at least some group membership involving systematic social relations. How else would it be possible to understand our experience? This, in Mead's view, was the primary objective of social psychology. He seeks to deal with experience 'from the social psychological standpoint of society', in which communication is essential:

> Social psychology, on this view, presupposes an approach to experience from the standpoint of the individual, but undertakes to determine in particular that which belongs to this experience because the individual himself belongs to a social structure, a social order. (Mead, 1934: 1)

Mead adds that social psychology is 'especially interested in the effect which the social group has in the determination of the experience and conduct of the individual member'.

So now we have some more precise terms by which to define the social context of learning. These are the social structure, the social order and the social group. We also have a more precise description of the Mead's perspective on the problems of mind and self. He called this social behaviourism:

> Psychology is not something that deals with consciousness; psychology deals with the experience of the individual in its relation to the conditions under which the experience goes on. It is social psychology where the conditions are social ones. It is behaviouristic where the approach to experience is made through conduct. (Mead, 1934: 40–41)

Any theory of learning associated with this view of mind and self as socially constructed, therefore, will be behaviouristic. However, in the case of Mead, behaviourism means something different from the common use of the term in psychology (see chapter 4). Instead, it is derived from the work of Dewey and philosophical pragmatism:

> You can get at your own conduct and at the conduct of other people by considering that conduct in an objective sort of fashion. That is what behaviouristic psychology is trying to do, trying to avoid the ambiguity of the term 'consciousness'. (Mead, 1977: 82)

Mead's approach to social psychology is naturalistic, scientific, behaviouristic and pragmatic. It attempts to locate consciousness, mind and self in the social process, structure or order.

What theory of learning emerges from all this? In the first place, learning is a matter of adaptation by way of habit and response:

> Learning consists in the modification of impulses and the transference of modified behaviour to various particulars 'belonging to the same class'. Thus learning means acquiring habitual ways of acting or habitual responses applicable to an indefinite number of situations and particulars. Intelligence, learning, and habit formation apply only to organisms having needs that can be fulfilled by behaving in certain ways toward, and acting on, objects in their respective environments. (Miller, 1973: 10)

But the environment of learning is social. We can only get evidence of learning through communication – by way of 'significant symbols' or language. In other words, we can only be said to learn in so far as we can share and communicate with others. For Mead, the whole concept of the 'self' depends upon the 'other'. This brings us back to a sociological concept of role which involves 'an awareness of sharable, socialized, habitualized responses and the corresponding objects to which they answer; and these responses are evoked by significant symbols or language gestures' (Miller, 1973: 17).

And so we return to what is, in essence, a sociological concept of learning. Mead fills in the detail of how socialization into an 'objectified culture' takes place: by concepts of the self and by social processes of symbolization and language. Learning therefore can only be social, because mind and self are themselves constructed through the social process of habit and response. In the end, much of this can be traced back to Darwinian evolution theory, from which early functionalist sociology itself emerged, later to be replaced by more interactive theories. Mead has had considerable influence on later developments in sociology, particularly those based on social interactionism in the 1960s (Mead, 1977: xiv). Social psychologists, however, have continued to develop social learning theory, and we now turn briefly to a modern example of this.

Bandura and social learning theory

As a theory, Albert Bandura's social learning theory lacks the sociological dimensions of role, structure and culture. However, he builds upon the kinds of social interactionism which Mead's own theory stressed:

> Social learning theory emphasizes the prominent roles played by vicarious, symbolic and self-regulatory processes in psychological functioning. (Bandura, 1977: vii)

Bandura accepts that, as a social process, learning involves functionalism, interactionism, and significant symbolism. But he stresses how far individuals are capable of self-regulation and self-direction. This brings learning theory into the service of one of the primary characteristics of lifelong learning theory (see chapters 1 and 2 of this book):

> Social learning theory approaches the explanation of human behaviour in terms of a continuous reciprocal interaction between cognitive, behavioural and environmental determinants. Within the process of reciprocal determinism lies the opportunity for people to influence their destiny as well as the limits of self-direction. This conception of human functioning then neither casts people into the role of powerless objects controlled by environmental forces nor free agents who can become whatever they choose. Both people and their environments are reciprocal determinants of each other. (Bandura, 1977: vii)

Bandura describes the social process, therefore, as one of reciprocal determination. He tries to show that 'people are not simply reactors to external influences'. Like Mead, Bandura adopts a behaviourist perspective, but one derived from social interaction theory rather than from stimulus-response learning theorists such as Watson and Pavlov. He stresses the symbolic and communicative aspects of human behaviour, together with individuals' capacity for self-regulatory control.

The theory of reciprocal determinism means that individual and environmental influences are interdependent. 'To take one example, people's expectations influence how they behave, and the outcomes of their behaviour change their expectations' (Bandura, 1977: 195). The implications for education are clear. Motivation to learn arises, or fails to, in a social context of mutual expectation by teachers and learners.

Bandura's social learning theory, therefore, develops the kind of themes introduced by Mead's earlier social psychology. However, it lacks an adequate social structural or cultural dimension. This means that, when he considers social control (Bandura, 1977: 208–13), he argues only that social learning theory does not entail social control. But his argument is conducted in a sociological vacuum. It conveys little sense of the symbolic significance of, for example, structural inequality. Divorced from critical social theory, social learning theory can be seen as serving the purposes of the 'lifestyle' market economy associated with postmodern society and theories (eg Brookfield, 1987) which celebrate individual choice and self-development.

> Psychology cannot tell people how they ought to live their lives. It can, however, provide them with the means for effecting personal and social change. And it can aid them in making value choices by assessing the consequences of alternatives lifestyles and institutional arrangements. (Bandura, 1977: 213)

Bandura's theory arises, however, in a context of psychological research into how individuals learn. It is based on concepts such as response, conditioning, stimulus, reward, imitation, conformity, deviance and so on, in relation to personality development (Bandura, 1963). Its concerns with personal and social change anticipate some of the underlying concerns of lifelong learning.

There is nothing in either Mead or Bandura's theories of social learning which addresses the issue of whether social groups, institutions or organizations can themselves be said to learn. What we have been looking at are theories, derived from evolutionism, sociology and social psychology, about the relation between the individual and the social in the learning process.

Obviously, social learning does not mean the same thing as collective learning, and we must at this point return to the questions posed at the beginning of this chapter.

Collective learning

Can social collectivities, such as families, communities, organizations or whole societies, be said to learn? This is an important issue. Today we often hear about the need to develop a 'learning society', a 'learning culture' or a 'learning organization'. These terms imply learning can take a more collective, and less individualistic, form. A learning organization, for instance, seems to mean more than just an organization in which lots of individuals learn.

Collective or group learning can be defined as learning which is more than the sum of the individual learning of the members of the group or organization. Groups and organizations exist in a wider environment, so several of the concepts introduced in this chapter can help us to understand the process of collective learning. For example, Darwinian evolution theory suggests that in a hostile (competitive) environment, organizations must adapt in order to survive. From a sociological or social psychological perspective, this can be seen as a learning process. The same can be said for groups or communities striving to achieve collective ends.

Such a learning process cannot be described just as socialization or response to the environment. It is a mutual, proactive process, in which the group or organization 'acts back' on the environment. A community group, for instance, may try to create a moral or political climate in which its aims are more likely to be achieved. A commercial organization will attempt to create a need amongst its customers or clients for its goods and services. Whether we call this a learning process depends on how we define 'collective' – as opposed to 'individual' or 'personal' – learning. Individuals are socialized into the culture of the organizations, learning how to belong to and function effectively within them. As we shall see in chapter 13, organizations are now often thought of as like living organisms, which must learn in order to survive. Some of these ideas are controversial because our ideas of learning continue to reflect an 'individualistic paradigm' at the same time as 'collective learning' is increasingly accepted as a useful way of analysing organizations.

Conclusion

In this chapter, we have introduced several kinds of social learning theory, from the sociological approach which stresses socialization, culture, role and structure, to notions of the mind and the self as themselves social constructs. The social context – through communication, language, symbolism and so on – is also of great significance to the learning process. Mead refers to the self and the 'other'; Bandura to reciprocal determinism; others say simply that learning cannot be anything other than social. In all these approaches, the relation between the individual and the group (or collectivity or society) is the constant factor.

Chapter 6

Experiential learning

Although in each of the previous chapters we have explored central ideas about learning, we have not yet given much attention to the experience of the learner. We do so in this chapter, because it has become a key feature of much contemporary thinking about adult learning. Even using the term 'experiential learning' can, however, be problematic, since, as Brah and Hoy (1989: 73) point out, the term has recently become something of an ideology in education. However, they also note correctly that learning from experience has a long history within education and stems from a number of traditions.

While retaining the term 'experiential learning', we want to focus much more deliberately upon experience in this chapter. We shall use the term rather as Brah and Hoy use the idea of learning from experience. But what matters is not that this may be a new orthodoxy, but how far it provides genuine insights into understanding how adults learn.

Miller and Boud (1996: 8–10) neatly summarize the underlying tenets of experiential learning as follows.

- Experience is the foundation of, and stimulus for, learning.
- Learners actively construct their own experience.
- Learning is holistic.
- Learning is socially and culturally constructed.
- Learning is influenced by the socio-economic context within which it occurs.

Experiential learning may be defined as the process of creating and transforming experience into knowledge, skills, attitudes, values, emotions, beliefs and senses. It is the process through which individuals become themselves.

A key feature to note is that many experientialists see experience itself as a social construct. We come to every situation with our own autobiographies, and we interpret the situation and consequently construct our experiences. This approach, known as constructivism, has become a major element in recent learning theory.

Brah and Hoy also rightly point to a number of different traditions which have used the idea – and in fact there are even more than those they mention. The whole history of progressive education has been student-centred and has tended to use the experience of learners. For Knowles (1980), using learners' experience is central to andragogy. Action learning (Revans, 1980) is also a form of experiential learning, as is problem-based learning (Barrows and Tamblyn, 1980). (Action learning and problem-based learning are discussed further in chapter 12.) It would be possible to point to the importance of using experience in many other well-known approaches to education and teaching (eg Freire, 1972). This supports Brah and Hoy's belief that experiential learning, in one form or another, has become a new orthodoxy.

As they point out, however, this is no new form of learning. Ancient writers recognized that this was how people learn. In the stories of Christ, for instance, the prodigal son 'came to himself' – or 'learnt from his experience'. Kant (1993: 30) opens his *Critique of Pure Reason* with the claim 'that all our knowledge begins with experience there can be no doubt'. Dewey's (1938) book focuses on the place of experience in education, and Lewin (1951) recognized the same truth. Kolb (1984) draws upon each of these later writers in building up his theory of experiential learning.

There are other writers, from a different tradition, who want to start with experience, although they use different terminology. Schön (1983) refers to reflection-in-action, Lave and Wenger (1991) use the term situated learning, and in a completely different way Belenky *et al.* (1986) point to women's ways of knowing. The widespread influence of this approach can be seen when we recall that Mezirow's (1991) transformative learning is based on the idea that the meaning schemes and perspectives which learners have on their experience are transformed.

Such a wealth of material led Weil and McGill (1989) to suggest that experiential learning might be classified into four categories which they called 'villages':

- assessment and accreditation of 'prior' experiential learning;
- experiential learning and change in post-school education and training;
- experiential learning and social change;
- personal growth and development.

This formulation is an attempt to demonstrate the breadth of current discussion about experiential learning. Yet discussion about the nature of experience itself is missing from a great deal of this work. Many people, even professionals, still do not focus upon their own experience in learning. Brookfield (1996: 27) writes that in recent years he has 'worked more and more with helping teachers take their experiences seriously so that they can begin the process of problem solving with collaborative and critical reflection on these experiences'.

Kolb, writing with Fry in 1975, tried to crystallize this discussion with a simple experiential learning cycle. This has subsequently become known as Kolb's Learning Cycle (see Figure 6.1).

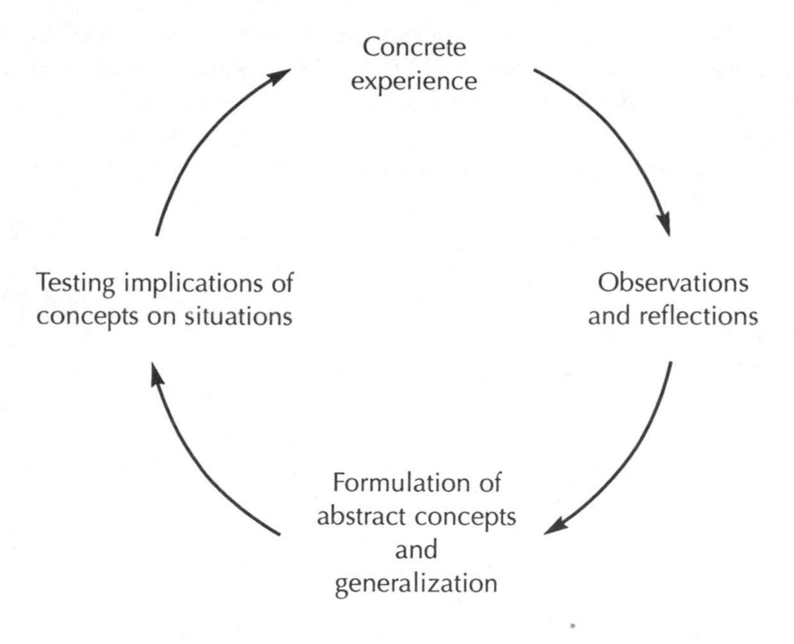

Figure 6.1 *An experiential learning cycle*

This diagram has probably become the most well known of all illustrations about learning. It tries to capture the heart of the experiential learning process, although it omits some of the stages and aspects of the process. Boud, Keogh and Walker (1985: 36) illustrated this by including feelings and emotions in the process.

Using Kolb's cycle as a starting point for his empirical research into how adults learn, Jarvis restructured Kolb's diagram to include more of the processes. His work has been more fully reported elsewhere and is only briefly mentioned here. His diagram (Figure 6.2) illustrates the process.

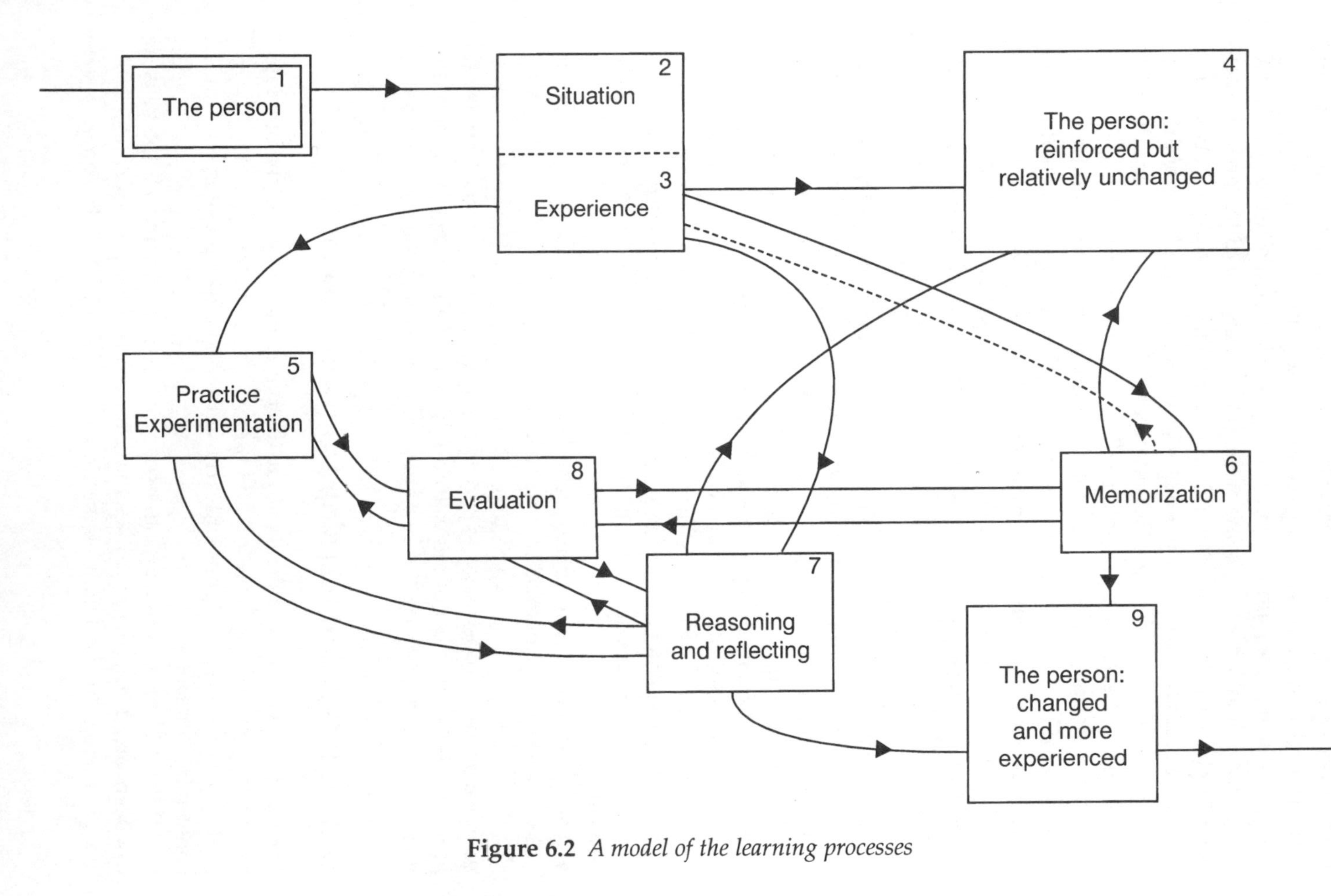

Figure 6.2 *A model of the learning processes*

In workshops, Jarvis invited participants to write down learning episodes in their own lives. He then asked them to compare their learning in pairs, and then 'snowballed' the pairs into groups of four. Having discussed their learning episodes, and drawn out some of the similarities and differences, he then asked each group to redraw Kolb's cycle to fit their four experiences. Each diagram contained variations on Kolb's cycle and the complexity of the learning processes began to emerge. He undertook this process with nine different workshops, and some two hundred participants, and Figure 6.2 is a composite of those discussions and reports. It remains an over-simplification of the learning processes that occur as a result of experience, but it does illustrate something of the complexity of experiential learning.

This diagram shows how individuals enter a situation and construct their experience. However, this simple sentence hides a multitude of significant points.

- Individuals are in part their own biographies. Jarvis thinks it important to distinguish biography from past experiences. Biography includes the hidden and unconscious, while past experience conveys the impression only of experiences of which we are conscious. For Knowles, however, using previous experiences was at the heart of andragogy.
- Individuals enter situations and construct experiences. But the experience they construct is one that either they themselves or others (perhaps a teacher or facilitator) create on their behalf. The situation itself, therefore, is only the context within which the experiences occurs, not the experience itself.
- The experience they have may be either primary or secondary, either actual or recalled, either real or artificial.

As a result of their constructed experience, individuals may or may not learn. Jarvis suggests a number of routes through this complex diagram, indicating different types of learning. These routes are described in the next section.

Different types of learning from experience

Perhaps the easiest way to demonstrate the routes mentioned in the previous section is by examining Table 6.1, and then describing each type of learning.

Each of the reflective forms of learning can have two possible outcomes: conformity or change.

All these forms of learning can occur simultaneously, and all the senses can be involved. This demonstrates the complexity of the processes which we are discussing. In the following sections, we describe briefly some of the

Table 6.1 *A typology of learning*

Category of response to experience	Type of learning/nonlearning
Non-learning	Presumption Non-consideration Rejection
Non-reflective learning	Preconscious learning Skills learning Memorization
Reflective learning	Contemplation Reflective skills learning Experimental learning

main routes through the learning diagram which are associated with the types of learning mentioned above.

Non-learning

People do not always learn from their experiences. This is why we start with a discussion of the non-learning responses to experience: presumption, non-consideration and rejection.

Presumption

Presumption is the typical response to everyday experience. It involves trusting that the world will not change and that successful actions can therefore be repeated effectively. This appears almost thoughtless and mechanical, but it is the basis of a great deal of social living. It would be quite intolerable for people to have to consider every word and every action in every social situation before they performed it. (For presumption, the route through Figure 6.2 is 1 to 4.)

Non-consideration

Non-consideration is another response to potential learning experiences that occurs commonly in everyday life. Its effect on the actors varies depending on the circumstances. People may not respond to a potential learning experience for a variety of reasons. They may be too busy to think about it, they may be fearful of the outcome, or they may be in no position to understand the situation. Thus, though they might recognize the potential for learning from the experience, they may be unable to respond to it. (For non-consideration, the route through Figure 6.2 is 1 to 4.)

Rejection

Some people have an experience but reject the possibility that they could learn from it. For instance, think of an older person (or a young one) experiencing the complexity of the modern city and exclaiming, 'I don't know what this world is coming to!' Here is a possible learning experience – an experience of the complex modern world – but instead of probing it and seeking to understand it, some individuals reject the possibility. Anyone who looks at the world and says they will not allow any of their opinions or attitudes to be changed regardless, because they are sure they are right, is in this situation. This is rejecting learning opportunities on principle. Rejection may actually serve to confirm them in positions they already hold. (For rejection, the route through Figure 6.2 is 1 to 3 to 7 to either 4 or 9.)

Sociologically, the significant thing about any response to experience is that no one is totally individuated. Everyone lives in a society. What, then, are the effects of non-learning? The most significant may be that when we reject the opportunity to learn, society and its structures cannot be affected by our experiences. (It may, however, be argued that any failure to affect the structures of society might hinder later changes, and that even non-action has consequences.) In addition, little change is likely to occur in the actors, because people's knowledge, skills and attitudes do not change when they do not learn.

There is a distinct advantage to this situation. People who tend to approach things presumptively, or without consideration, experience considerable freedom, because their life unfolds as they expect. This sense of freedom results from the fact that society does not seem to be pressuring them to do anything they do not want to do.

Non-reflective learning

The three types of learning that constitute non-reflective learning – preconscious learning, skills learning and memorization – are the types usually thought of as learning proper. They share the feature that they do not involve reflectivity.

Preconscious learning

Preconscious learning is often called incidental learning, although preconscious and incidental learning are in fact very different. Incidental learning may well be conscious but its occurrence is still incidental. Preconscious learning occurs at the edge of consciousness, or at the periphery of what we see with our eyes. Typically, individuals monitor their actions, albeit with a low level of consciousness, and memorize them. Drivers are not usually conscious of all the incidents that occur during a journey, but when answering a specific question, they may respond, 'I think I vaguely recall something like that.' If pressed, they may recall something quite specific. They have learnt, but the learning has not necessarily become conscious knowledge.

Preconscious learning is not likely to occur as a result of experiencing in the communicative mode. It can, however, take place if the two modes of experience (see the section on the nature of experience later in this chapter) occur simultaneously and the recipient concentrates on the secondary rather than the primary experience. For instance, in conversations people may not concentrate on their environment, but may see things from the 'corner of their eye', or be 'vaguely aware' that something else is happening while they speak. (For preconscious learning, the route through Figure 6.2 is 1 to 3 to 6 to 4.)

Skills learning

Skills learning is usually associated with such activities as training for a manual occupation, or the acquisition of a high level of physical fitness through training. But some learning in preparation for manual tasks should certainly not be described as non-reflective. Thus this term has to be further restricted to the learning of simple, short procedures, such as those that somebody on an assembly line might be taught. These skills are often acquired through imitation and role modelling.

Skills learning is another form of learning that occurs in the action mode of experience rather than in communicative interaction. There is a significant relationship between skills learning and knowledge. Learners may watch a demonstration and then claim that they know how to carry out a task. However, they only know cognitively and indirectly (through memorization), until they have actually performed the task for themselves. (For skills learning, the route through Figure 6.2 is 1 to 3 to 5 to 8 to 6 to either 4 or 9.)

Memorization

Memorization is probably the most commonly known form of learning. Children learn their mathematical tables, their language vocabularies and so on by memorization. When adults return to higher education, they may feel that this is the most important type of learning. They may try to memorize what their instructor says, or what some scholar has written, in order to reproduce it in an examination. The authority speaks and every word of wisdom must be learnt and memorized. Memorization can also occur as a result of past successful acts. Memories are stored away and form the basis of planning future actions. Thus, memorization also relates to direct action experiences. (For memorization, the route through Figure 6.2 is 1 to 3 to 6, then possibly to 8 to 6, and then to either 4 or 9.)

In the wider social context, preconscious learning, skills learning and memorization represent a process of social reproduction. Society and its structures remain unquestioned and unaltered. When people learn in this way, they learn to fit into the larger organization or the wider society. They are, as it were, learning their place.

Reflective learning

We have seen that learning tends to be culturally reproductive, simply because that is the way it is frequently defined. We have suggested that non-reflective learning inevitably reproduces prevailing social structures. This is not true of the three types of reflective learning: contemplation, reflective skills learning and experimental learning.

Contemplation

Contemplation is a common form of learning which behaviourist definitions of learning do not allow for. It is a very intellectual approach to learning, because it involves pure thought. Contemplation is the process of thinking about an experience and reaching a conclusion about it without necessarily referring to a wider social reality. Contemplation (the word, with its religious overtones, is carefully chosen) can involve not only meditation but also the reasoning processes of the philosopher or theorist, the activities of the pure mathematician, and even the thought processes of everyday life. What distinguishes contemplative learning from the process of thinking itself is the fact that in the former case a conclusion is reached. (For contemplation, the route through Figure 6.2 is 1 to 3 to 7 to 8 to 6 to 9, with two-way processes operating throughout the latter part of this path.)

Reflective skills learning

In an earlier book, Jarvis (1987: 34–5) referred to reflective skills learning as reflective practice. This is one of the forms of learning that Schön (1983) had in mind when he pointed out that professionals in practice tend to think on their feet. In responding to unique situations, they often produce new skills. In fact, many skills are learnt in a totally unthinking manner, so reflective skills learning may be regarded as a more sophisticated approach to learning practical subjects. It involves not only learning a skill but also learning the concepts that underpin the practice. This makes it possible to know why the skill should be performed in a specific way. (For reflective skills learning, the route through Figure 6.2 is 1 to 3 to 5, 7, and 8 and then loop as many times as necessary in both directions out from 5 to 8 to 6 to 9.)

Experimental learning

In experimental learning, theory is tried out in practice. The result is a new form of knowledge that captures social reality. This approach to learning demonstrates how individuals are always thinking and devising new practical knowledge for themselves in every walk of life. (For experimental learning, the route through Figure 6.2 is 1 to 3 to 7, 5, and 8 and then loop as many times as necessary in both directions out from 7 to 8 to 6 to 9.)

These three forms of learning – non-learning, non-reflective, and reflective – are, of course, not always innovative. The word 'learning' can be used to denote both conformist and innovative outcomes. This can seem paradoxical. Learning can result in agreement and conformity, or in disagreement and innovation. The second set of outcomes makes a consideration of power crucial to any understanding of learning.

All forms of experiential learning can be behavioural, action-based, cognitive or social. All of these can also occur simultaneously, since experience itself has many dimensions. In other words, experiential learning is a much more comprehensive theory of learning, and not surprisingly it has become something of a new orthodoxy. Indeed, it demonstrates many of the points made in chapter 1 about the recent changes development in late modern, or postmodern, society.

However, we have not yet discussed the nature of the experience, and how it is used in learning. We undertake this task in the following sections.

The nature of experience

Philosophers have long focused on the concept of experience. Oakeshott (1933: 9) saw experience as among the most difficult words in the philosophical vocabulary to manage. We do not try here to define the concept, but to see how experience is used in learning situations. We shall do this by examining a number of scenarios: everyday life, didactic classroom education, student-centred classroom education and workplace learning. In order to do so, it is necessary to examine the ideas of primary or secondary, actual or recalled, and real or artificial experience. Every experience of course is in some sense 'real', even though it may be indirect or mediated, so these six terms are by no means mutually exclusive.

- *Primary experience*. This is an experience by any, or all, of the senses of aspects of the social context within which the experience occurs.
- *Secondary experience*. This is a mediated experience having little or nothing to do with the social context within which the experience occurs, such as a video presentation or even a theoretical discussion.
- *Actual experience*. This is an experience that occurs at the present time.
- *Recalled experience*. This is the process of recalling memories of previous actual experiences.
- *Real experience*. This is an experience of the actual context.
- *Artificial experience*. This is a created form of experience, highlighting some aspects of other real or actual experiences.

It should be noted that Jarvis' use of biography and Knowles' use of past experiences refer to the sum total of experiences that have helped to shape a human person. Memory, on the other hand, refers to consciously recalled experiences.

It is now possible to discuss the different forms of experiential learning.

Experiential learning in everyday life

Everyday life takes place in, and relates to, people's social contexts. In the process of experiencing in all its modes, people learn – sometimes deliberately but often incidentally. Experiential learning in everyday life is almost synonymous with conscious living. This is how people learn naturally and it has become the model for other forms of experiential learning.

Didactic classroom education

In teacher-centred education, teachers sometimes ignore their students' previous experiences and assume almost that they are empty vessels to be filled with information. It is worth recalling that the classroom context is the primary experience and the information being provided is only secondary. The didactic education that takes place within the classroom is based on the provision of secondary experiences. As such it often seems far removed from everyday life. Only in story telling does the story teller try to relate the story to the experiences of the listeners. Whilst the experiences of listening to the story are secondary, the story seeks to encourage listeners to recall similar experiences from their own lives and to empathize with the characters in the story.

Student-centred classroom learning

There is a variety of different approaches to student-centred learning. All endeavour to use students' past, or recalled, experiences and to provide primary and/or artificial experiences from which they may continue to learn. For instance, in many forms of problem-based learning, the teacher (or facilitator) selects an actual problem from 'real life' and presents it in the artificial context of the classroom to be solved by the class. In role-play, the teacher or facilitator provides an actual primary experience, in the artificial context of the classroom, which relates to the type of experience that the role-players may have in 'real life'. In classroom discussions, teachers may ask students to recall actual experiences and focus on them, in order to share with their fellow students what they have learnt from those recalled experiences.

There are also courses, such as teacher-training, where there is some workplace learning. The course therefore provides actual, real experiences as part of the professional preparation. Finally, in continuing education, practitioners who return to the classroom are frequently asked to recall their work experiences, reflect on them and learn from them.

Workplace learning

With ever more rapid changes in the nature of work, the workplace has come to be seen as a place where learning occurs. Work-based learning, action learning and so on are all part of this process. It is recognized that work itself provides potential learning experiences, with none of the artificiality of the classroom attached. In a rapidly changing world, the workplace has therefore become an important site for learning and for new forms of continuing education programme.

Limitations of experiential learning

A great deal of our knowledge of the world cannot be gained from primary experience. Secondary experiences have therefore to be provided. As the world has become a smaller place, for instance, we are more aware of events in all corners of the globe – but we cannot have primary experiences of them all. Additionally, when we are learning new subjects, we need to be told about them before we can experience them. We need to be told that certain things are unsafe, so that we never actually experience them. Theory is provided through secondary experience, since we cannot experience knowledge through our senses. Many forms of initial training for jobs have devised curricula that seek to include more primary experiences (see, eg Schön, 1987).

Consequently, although experiential learning in all its forms may have become a new orthodoxy, there are many situations when we have to learn from secondary and mediated experience. In these cases, we have to recognize that we are learning from other people's experiences and interpretations. These must be assessed critically before we accept them. But without learning from secondary experiences, our knowledge of the world would be greatly impoverished.

Conclusion

The recognition of human experience as a basis for learning, then, is nothing new. As the mystique of scientific experiment declines, however, it is possible to remove learning research from the laboratory and return it to its original basis in human experience. While all the scientific studies of learning are valid, they all find their place in this wider understanding of the human processes of learning from experience. Education, as we know it today, is a product of modernity. We are beginning to recognize that some of the values of the age are now open to question. Human experience is becoming central to a great deal more of teaching and learning – but we still need, and are enriched by, learning from secondary experiences.

Chapter 7

Types of learning

In the first part of this book, we explored a number of different theories of human learning. While we have not exhausted them all, we have tried to demonstrate the extent of research which has been devoted to trying to understand these processes. Needless to say, different authors have used different terminology to describe the types of learning that they have studied. In this very brief chapter we try to show how many of the different terms they use refer to very similar phenomena. The chapter falls into two parts. In the first, we discuss the terminology used by various authors. In the second, we endeavour to synthesize some of the types of learning discussed.

Authors and their terminology

For ease of reference, in this discussion we list authors in alphabetical order rather than according to the school of thought from which they emerge.

C Argyris and D Schön

In 1974, these two authors adopted the distinction, originally drawn by Ashby (1952), between single-loop and double-loop learning. Argyris and Schön (1974: 19) defined these terms in the following way:

> In single-loop learning, we learn to maintain the field of constancy by learning to design actions that satisfy existing governing variables. In double-loop learning, we learn to change the field of constancy itself.

We can make sense of this as follows. Suppose a situation is in harmony and then something destroys it. In single-loop learning, we learn to solve the problem and adjust our behaviour without changing the situation itself. With double-loop learning, we ask questions about the situation which caused the need to adjust our behaviour. It is in effect the difference between problem solving and problematizing the situation within which the problem emerged. The work of Argyris and Schön is discussed in chapter 13.

J Botkin *et al.*

In a report to the Club of Rome in 1979, Botkin, Elmandjra and Malitza (1979: 10) suggested that there are two fundamental types of learning: maintenance and innovative. They defined maintenance learning as:

> the acquisition of fixed outlooks, methods, and rules for dealing with known and recurring situations. It enhances our problem-solving ability for problems that are given. It is the type of learning designed to maintain an existing system or an established way of life.

They contrasted this type of learning with innovative learning. They saw the latter as even more essential in contemporary society since it could 'bring change, renewal, restructuring and problem reformulation' (1979: 10). However, they felt that a great deal of innovative learning occurred only as a result of crisis, and they considered this a problem in a rapidly changing world. Consequently, they argued that innovative learning should be anticipatory and participatory. They called for an ethos that encouraged people to play their part, as autonomous and responsible members of society in all its facets. Unfortunately, this far-reaching report never received the publicity it deserved.

Stephen Brookfield

A great deal of Brookfield's writing has focused upon learning and thinking. Since 1987, he has written quite extensively about critical thinking. He suggests (1987: 7–9) four components of critical thinking:

- recognizing and challenging assumptions;
- challenging the importance of the context;
- being willing to explore alternatives;
- becoming reflectively sceptical.

In a sense, he does not contrast this with anything in the present book. In his earlier writing (eg 1986) he does not place as much emphasis on criticality; indeed, he is more concerned about facilitating the learning process. However, there is always an implicit contrast with non-critical learning. For Brookfield, criticality does not mean disagreeing, but being willing to question a situation or information, rather than to accept it. It is similar to reflective thinking; non-critical thinking is similar to non-reflective thinking.

Paulo Freire

From his very earliest writing (1972 translations), Freire maintained a distinction between what he called 'banking education' and 'problem-posing education'. This resulted in two types of learning. In 'banking education', learners were expected to remember and repeat what they were taught. In 'problem-posing education', they were encouraged to question situations and learn from their questioning. In the former, they accepted the situation and the status quo and their learning occurred within that context, while in the latter they were encouraged to question the validity of the situation. Freire uses the term 'problem posing' rather than 'problem solving' since, in his view, the latter term still accepts the status quo. We shall discuss this point more fully in the second part of this chapter. Freire saw this in political terms: it was only through problem-posing education that learners could become empowered to act in their own interests.

Peter Jarvis

As described in chapter 6, Jarvis (1987; 1992) distinguishes between non-reflective and reflective learning. In addition, he also introduces a category of non-learning. All learning and some elements of non-learning begin with situations where there is a disjuncture between a learner's biography (past experiences) and their construction of present experience. Non-reflective learning is just the process of accepting what is being presented and memorizing or repeating it, or accepting a situation within which an experience occurs and learning from it. In contrast, reflective learning is the process of being critical. This can mean thinking about the situation (and/or what is presented) and then deciding to accept or seek to change the situation. It can also involve accepting or seeking to change the information which has been presented.

Although his own research was with adults, Jarvis does not distinguish reflective and non-reflective learning according to age. He recognizes that children may also be reflective learners, and that adults are often non-reflective learners.

Malcolm Knowles

Knowles (1980: 43) made the classic distinction between andragogy and pedagogy in 1970, although he was later forced to reformulate it. He wrote that originally his distinction was as follows:

> Andragogy [is] the art and science of helping adults learn, in contrast to pedagogy [which is] the art and science of teaching children.

His distinction between adults and children was much criticized. Knowles' main concern, however, was that andragogy allowed learners the freedom to use their own experience and learn from the situations within which they found themselves. Pedagogy, on the other hand, in his view involved making learners learn what they were being taught by their teachers. He later accepted that school children are sometimes taught by student-centred methods and that adults are sometimes taught by teacher-centred methods. Knowles did not really understand school education: his concern was always with andragogy, in the way that he defined it.

Jack Mezirow

Mezirow (1991) made two sets of distinctions of interest in this chapter. The first came quite early in his study when he wrote that the 'formative learning of childhood becomes transformative learning in adulthood' (1991: 3). He states quite specifically that children accept their learning from sources of authority and that their early learning is socialization. Adults on the other hand need to acquire new meaning perspectives. In a sense, he makes here the same type of false distinction that Knowles made in 1970 between andragogy and pedagogy.

More significantly, Mezirow has been strongly influenced by Habermas' (1972) three processes of inquiry (technical, practical and emancipatory), and by his later writings on communicative action (Habermas, 1984). Mezirow (1991: 72–89) drew a threefold distinction between types of learning: instrumental, communicative and emancipatory. Instrumental learning 'involves determining cause–effect relationships and learning through task-orientated problem solving' (Mezirow, 1991: 73). Communicative learning is the process of 'learning to understand what others mean and to make ourselves understood' (Mezirow, 1991: 75). It involves negotiation with others through language and gesture and by anticipating the actions of others, so that it is 'designative as opposed to prescriptive… [which is] found in instrumental learning' (Mezirow, 1991: 79). Emancipatory learning involves identifying and challenging distorted meaning perspectives (Mezirow, 1991: 87) through a process of critical self-reflection (Mezirow, 1990). However, in one sense emancipatory learning need not be seen as distinct from the other two. Mezirow clearly seeks to distinguish between the designative and the prescriptive, although he recognizes that they may occur simultaneously.

A process of synthesis

In the above section we have seen how different scholars use very different terms to describe what are, fundamentally, the same sets of processes. Put rather crudely, learning either reinforces the status quo or changes some aspects of it. This section is therefore divided into two sub-sections.

Learning that reinforces the status quo

In Table 7.1 we see the different terminology used by these scholars for this type of learning, which each describes differently. It should be noted that some scholars still recognize that learners may be changed by a learning experience, even though it has no obvious effect on the situation within which the learning occurred.

Table 7.1 *Learning and the status quo*

Scholar	Terms used
Argyris and Schön	Single-loop learning
Botkin *et al.*	Maintenance learning
Brookfield	Not discussed – implicitly non-critical learning
Freire	Banking education
Jarvis	Non-reflective learning Reflective learning
Knowles	Pedagogy
Mezirow	Formative learning Instrumental learning

Argyris and Schön, Botkin *et al.* and Freire are basically concerned about the situation within which the learning occurs and regard this as unchanging. Jarvis and Mezirow, on the other hand, are both constructivists and recognize that learners construct their experiences in engaging with the social situations which they experience. For Jarvis, reflective learning does not automatically result in change, and so it is included in both Tables 7.1 and 7.2.

Learning and change

The potential for change was recognized by all the writers in the above section, although they again use different terminology to reflect what they are describing (see Table 7.2).

Table 7.2 *Learning and change*

Scholar	Terms used
Argyris and Schön	Double-loop learning
Botkin *et al.*	Innovative learning
Brookfield	Critical learning
Freire	Problem-posing education
Jarvis	Reflective learning
Knowles	Andragogy
Mezirow	Transformative learning Emancipatory learning

Two types of change can occur as a result of the learning process. First, the learners may be changed. Second, they may act to change the situation within which they function. All the writers accept that the learners might be changed by the learning process, although Mezirow is the one who focuses most on the meaning perspectives of the learners. All, apart from Knowles, discuss the fact that the learners might not accept either the situation from which they learn or the information they are presented with to learn from. All recognize that changed learners might become change agents as a result of the learning process, and may be emancipated from being trapped in their situations.

It is at this point – what action follows learning – that the political dimension arises. Such action might question the status quo. Learning *per se* is amoral (Jarvis, 1997); that is, it is neither good nor bad in itself, but merely a human process that occurs all the time. But the outcomes of learning do have moral consequences. They affect the learners, the situation within which they act, and the people with whom they interact. Learning is, therefore, always potentially dangerous. It can raise questions about or disturb the status quo in society. This is why so much of it has been institutionalized and controlled by the state, churches and now, to some extent, by sectors of society such as industry and commerce.

It is, therefore, interesting today to find learning being used as if it is always good and beneficial to society. The UNESCO World Conference in Hamburg in 1997, for instance, was entitled 'Learning – the Key to the Twenty-first Century'. Knowledge is changing rapidly, so learning is now needed in order to keep abreast with the social change. In order to be competitive in the global market, countries must insure that their knowledge-based industries are really at the 'cutting edge'. Consequently, the more dangerous elements in the learning process are being controlled in other ways. One element of this is the continued emphasis on vocationalism and the need for vocational qualifications. Another is the downplaying of the Humanities and some of the Social Sciences. Change has become change in the organization and its practices and procedures, rather than a wider questioning about society itself.

Conclusion

The ambivalent implications of the learning processes can be detected in the language used by the various scholars we have discussed. Learning in itself is an individual process, or set of processes. But no person is an island, and change always has social consequences. The fewer the consequences of learning for the social group, for example if the status quo is retained, the easier it may be for social harmony and cohesion. But, without change, the potential of the individual learners is inhibited. When there is freedom to learn, learners have more freedom to develop their potential – but since it is potentially innovative, this can sometimes be problematic for social groups.

Chapter 8

Culture and learning

Introduction

As earlier chapters have shown, what we know about learning has changed a good deal in recent years. We no longer think of learning simply in terms of what behavioural changes take place. Neither do we see it just as a matter of the processing of information in people's brains. Rather, we now think of learning as a social activity. Learners learn when they engage with knowledge in social contexts. But learners also learn when they engage with things which we might not usually think of as 'knowledge'. For example, we learn when we engage with other people's beliefs (or, as we may think, their prejudices).

Very broadly, the process of learning is about making sense of experiences which we have. These may be formal education or training, of course, but we can also learn in other ways: watching television, reading newspapers, gardening, shopping at supermarkets, funerals, family crises, getting drunk and playing golf. What matters, however, is not just the experience, but how we interpret that experience.

If we take this view, it is apparent that 'learning' is likely to vary, depending on where, how and why it is taking place, and who is doing the learning. If social context influences learning, what and how people learn is likely to be different in different cultural and social contexts. This represents something of a challenge to traditional views of learning and teaching, where the quest has too often been for 'the' theory of learning.

The problem is that culture is a very complex phenomenon. Whole academic disciplines (sociology, anthropology and social history, for example), are largely devoted to understanding what cultures are and how they change. 'Cultural studies' itself is now a well-established field of intellectual inquiry.

So far as learning is concerned, it is much easier to say that culture is very important than to describe exactly what the impact of different cultures is. This is partly because learning is very closely connected not only to culture, but also to knowledge. What and how we learn are influenced by culture; but culture must be learnt. What counts as knowledge differs between cultural contexts.

However, some very interesting and important research has been conducted in recent years. In this chapter, we provide some illustration of the insights which this work has given us. It is worth saying at the outset that it has not yet provided simple solutions or models. Probably it never will. But if we have no simple answers, we do now know a good deal more about what questions we should be asking.

We look in some depth at important contributions to research in two areas. We could have discussed others, such as learning in later life and learning among ethnic minorities in western countries. However, we feel that it is more useful to examine topics in some depth. We therefore begin with research on women's learning. Then we look at an important recent contribution on learning in Chinese societies.

How do women learn?

When Malcolm Knowles introduced his concept of 'andragogy', he wanted to develop a theory of learning and teaching appropriate to adults. Andragogy, he said, is the 'art and science of helping adults learn'. The more common term, 'pedagogy' referred to the 'art and science of teaching children' (Knowles, 1980: 43). As we have seen (chapter 7), Knowles thought children learnt, and should be taught, in very different ways from adults.

But adults are simply adults. According to Elias (1979: 254), no one suggested that 'the art and science of teaching women differs from the art and science of teaching men'. By the 1970s and 1980s some people were arguing just that. The modern women's movement was in its infancy when Knowles first wrote about andragogy (1970), but under its influence ideas, perspectives and research developed which went to the heart of this issue.

Concerns about gender in education first emerged in relation to the experiences of girls at school. As early as the mid-1960s, for instance, Kemener contrasted adjectives typically used to describe good male and female students. Where males might be commended for being 'active', 'adventurous', 'energetic', 'curious' or 'inventive', females would be praised for being 'appreciative', 'considerate', 'cooperative', 'poised', 'sensitive' or 'dependable' (quoted Fraser, 1995: 28).

Fraser points to the similarity between the adjectives used to describe good male behaviour and Knowles' view of what it means to be adult:

> When people define themselves as adults... they see themselves as producers or doers... They see themselves as being able to make their own decisions and face the consequences, to manage their own lives. (Knowles, 1980; quoted Fraser, 1995: 29)

We could make a similar case in relation to other influential w itings in adult learning. Maslow has been a central point of reference for much North American learning literature. The idea of 'self-directed learning' relies very heavily on his perspectives, for instance (Brockett and Hiemstra, 1991). Yet Maslow wrote of 'self-actualization' as though the human race consists of a multitude of broadly similar selves. Though each is unique, all (male and female – and come to that, Cantonese, Canadian, Pakistani and Peruvian) move along a common self-actualizing trajectory (Maslow, 1968). As Fraser remarks, 'Adult learning models are usually predicated on the assumption that the masculine norm and the adult norm are one and the same' (1995: 21).

Adult learning models have been based on sexist assumptions at least partly because research has made little attempt to explore whether there is anything special about how women learn. It was not until the late 1970s that feminist critique of psychology and learning theory began to be reflected in serious research. Two major contributions have now established a basis for debate.

Women's identity and morality: the work of Carol Gilligan

Carol Gilligan investigated women's personalities, taking a feminist perspective on developmental psychology. She argued (1982) that profound differences exist between the development of males and females. While for most writers people are seen as growing progressively more independent in their relationships with others, Gilligan argues that this pattern does not apply to women. Women, she says, find their identity within their relationships with others.

The origins of this difference may lie in different experiences of parenting. While girls are typically parented chiefly by a parent of the same sex, boys are not. Boys' identities are thus formed in a process of differentiation and separation from their primary carer, while girls' are formed within an awareness of similarity. As a result,

> relationships, and particularly issues of dependency, are experienced differently by women and men. For boys and men, separation and individuation are critically tied to gender identity, since separation from the mother is essential for the development of masculinity. For girls and women, issues of femininity or feminine identity do not depend on the achievement of separation from the mother or on the progress of individuation. Since masculinity is defined

> through separation while femininity is defined through attachment, male gender identity is threatened by intimacy while female gender identity is threatened by separation. Thus males tend to have difficulty with relationships, while females tend to have problems with individuation. (Gilligan, 1982: 8)

Gilligan explores the consequences of this for our understanding of the psychology of personal development. She argues that girls and women develop a morality based on ideas of care and responsibility, which contrasts with that developed by boys and men, based on rights. A rights morality seeks abstract laws and universal principles which will settle disputes impartially, impersonally and fairly. (This has been described most influentially by Kohlberg; but Gilligan (1982: 18) criticizes Kohlberg for building a theory about how people's moral judgement develops on the basis of research based on a sample consisting only of males. Kohlberg's work has been discussed in chapter 4.)

The (typically, though not exclusively, female) morality of care and responsibility rejects the idea of blind impartiality. What individuals need cannot be worked out from universal rules and principles. Rather, in any situation of conflict, moral choices are to be worked out from the particular needs and experiences of each participant, 'on the premise of non-violence – that no one should be hurt' (Gilligan, 1982: 174). This can be done through dialogue, which allows each individual to be understood, and leads to understanding and consensus.

At first sight, this may all seem remote from learning. It is in fact central. Gilligan shows that women's development is different from men's. Much of learning theory has been based on the idea that all humans develop through various stages. Gilligan's work demolishes a universal notion of 'maturity', based on sexist (male) perceptions of what makes an autonomous, 'self-directed' person. She shows that many women (and some men) value relationships and mutuality above rights and autonomy, and that this can be seen not as a failing but as an alternative, and in some respects superior, morality. Morality must be learnt: Gilligan shows that men and women tend to learn different moralities, and she explains why.

Last, Gilligan shows that much of the previous literature has drawn conclusions about people in general from research based only on males, and this is as true of education and training as of psychology. And she shows that the articulation of a 'women's' morality can throw new light on our understanding of morality more generally.

Women's ways of knowing

One way of looking at Gilligan's work is to see it as showing how women's selves are formed through involvement in various (chiefly informal) learning processes in particular social contexts. She also shows that these forms of learning generate knowledge, and she asserts that this knowledge is of general significance (rather than just a 'women's concern'). Four other American researchers, Belenky, Clinchy, Goldberger and Tarule, tried to build on this approach by investigating the development of what they called 'women's ways of knowing'. They argued that 'conceptions of knowledge and truth... have been shaped throughout history by the male-dominated majority culture' (Belenky *et al.*, 1986: 5), and that:

> Relatively little attention has been given to modes of learning, knowing and valuing that may be specific to, or at least common in, women. It is likely that the commonly accepted stereotype of women's thinking as emotional, intuitive and personalized has contributed to the devaluation of women's minds and contributions, particularly in Western technologically oriented cultures, which value rationalism and objectivity. (Belenky *et al.*, 1986: 6)

Belenky and her colleagues interviewed at length some 135 'rural and urban American women of different ages, class and ethnic backgrounds, and educational histories' (Belenky *et al.*, 1986: 4), asking them questions about 'self-image, relationships of importance, education and learning, real-life decision-making and moral dilemmas, accounts of personal changes and growth, perceived catalysts for change and impediments to growth, and visions of the future' (Belenky *et al.*, 1986: 11). In a complex but rewarding book, they extended Gilligan's argument that women have a more relational orientation, which tends to generate a moral perspective distinct from men's.

They found that women used a distinct language to describe their intellectual and ethical development, based on metaphors of speaking and listening:

> In describing their lives, women commonly talked about voice and silence: 'speaking up', 'speaking out', 'being silenced', 'not being heard', 'really listening', 'really talking', 'words as weapons', 'feeling deaf and dumb', 'having no words', 'saying what you mean', 'listening to be heard' and so on, in an endless variety of connotations all having to do with sense of mind, self-worth, and feelings of isolation from or connection to others. We found that women repeatedly used the metaphor of voice to depict their intellectual and ethical development; and that the development of a sense of voice, mind and self were intricately intertwined. (Belenky *et al.*, 1986: 18)

Belenky and her colleagues contrasted this language of speaking and listening with the metaphor of vision which predominates in Western intellectual thought. Visual metaphors, they argue, encourage standing back to get a clear view of an object; listening involves being nearby, and registering subtle changes. 'Unlike seeing, speaking and listening suggest dialogue and interaction.' (Belenky *et al.*, 1986: 18)

Women's intellectual and moral development can be seen, according to Belenky and her colleagues, as proceeding through various 'ways of knowing'. They clearly see movement through these as progress or advance, though they do not suggest that every woman makes this progression. The five ways of knowing (Belenky *et al.*, 1986) are as follows.

Silence

This is a condition of ignorance, of unknowing, rather than knowing. For 'silent' women, speech is a weapon associated with acts of violence, and used without reason. Authorities do not use words to communicate thoughts or shared meanings. Women in this condition are passive, subdued and subordinate. Language is only useful to 'keep yourself out of trouble'. So although 'silent' women speak, they do not use language for constructive thought or communication, nor do they see it as a route to self-knowledge. Since the key feature which distinguishes women's ways of knowing from men's is speaking and listening, this condition of 'silence' is extreme (and, in the Belenky *et al.* study at least, also extremely rare).

Received knowledge

In contrast to the 'silent' (who are unaware of the power of words), words are central to the knowing process for women who rely on received knowledge. They learn by listening. But they have little confidence in their ability to speak. Truth comes from others. They are relieved when a friend says what they themselves think, but they see authorities as the source of truth. Because such women see all knowledge as originating outside the self, they look to others for self-knowledge. Unhappy with paradox or ambiguity, they seek a single right answer, and it must come instantly. They have no notion 'of understanding as a process taking place over time and demanding the exercise of reason' (Belenky *et al.*, 1986: 42). And because they do not see themselves as growing or evolving, they tend to be left behind in a rapidly changing technological society.

Subjective knowledge

For many women, moving away from silence and an externally oriented conception of knowledge and truth is achieved through 'a new conception of truth as personal, private, and subjectively known or intuited' (Belenky *et al.*, 1986: 54). This is personally liberating: a breaking away from external authority, producing a sense of optimism and strength. The truth is not 'out there', but inside you. The shift to this perspective on knowing is often associated with changes in personal life (such as having a child), and seems to be more often a matter of finding previously unknown inner resources than of a formal educational experience. Since (as Gilligan and others argue) women define themselves in terms of their relationships, breaking with previous relationships can lead to 'considerable flux in self-concept' (Belenky *et al.*, 1986: 81).

Subjectivists tend to discount others – and in particular remote experts – as sources of knowledge or advice: 'if they listen at all to others, it is to those who are most like themselves in terms of life experiences' (Belenky *et al.*, 1986: 68). One result of this is that, particularly in technological societies, subjectivists are disadvantaged when they have to go about learning and working in the public domain.

Procedural knowledge

Women arrive at procedural knowledge when their old ways of knowing – typically a mixture of received and subjectivist – are challenged. Procedural knowledge involves recognizing that truth is not revealed, but achieved through procedures, skills and techniques. It must be ferreted out through 'conscious, deliberate, systematic analysis' (Belenky *et al.*, 1986: 93). Lacking the certainties of external or internal authority, the 'inner voice turns critical'. Women in this position 'think before they speak; and because their ideas must measure up to certain objective standards, they speak in measured terms' (Belenky *et al.*, 1986: 94). Furthermore, they see truth as complex, and achieved through procedures which involve communication with others through talk. The views of others matter: not only what others think, but how they formed their opinions. This makes procedural knowledge 'more objective than subjective knowledge' (Belenky *et al.*, 1986: 98), and procedural knowers well-fashioned for practical, problem-solving tasks.

There are two sorts of procedural knowledge. Separate knowers play 'the game of impersonal reason'. Characteristic features of this are doubting, critical thinking and assuming everyone (including themselves) may be wrong. This is a traditionally male approach (according to Belenky *et al.*), and few women find argument ('reasoned critical discourse') entirely congenial. But for separate knowers authority lies in laws, rules, and reason, rather than in individuals, power or status. 'Disinterested reason is, of course, one of the highest human achievements,... [but for] some of the young women we interviewed... it degenerates into absence of interest, anomie, and monotony.' (Belenky *et al.*, 1986: 110)

Connected knowers, on the other hand, build on the subjectivist conviction that personal experience provides the best knowledge. They construct procedures for gaining access to other people's knowledge: these are based on the capacity for empathy. Accepting that this has limits, they act as 'connected rather than separate selves, seeing the other [person] not in their own terms but in the other's terms' (Belenky *et al.*, 1986: 113). Thus the knower gains 'vicarious (second-hand, firsthand) experience' (Belenky *et al.*, 1986: 115). A major source of such knowledge is conversation: gossip, which 'proceeds from trust and builds trust' (Belenky *et al.*, 1986: 116), can be important;

but so too can more formal collaboration in groups – but these must be long-standing in order to provide the basis for trust and shared inquiry.

Constructed knowledge

'All knowledge is constructed, and the knower is an intimate part of the known.' (Belenky *et al.*, 1986: 137) This is the essence of constructivist thought. Constructivists realize that questions and answers vary depending on historical and cultural context, and on the inquirer's frame of reference. Posing questions and problems become key methods of inquiry. Procedural knowers remain 'subservient to disciplines and systems' (Belenky *et al.*, 1986: 140), but constructivists search for truths beyond and across systems. They 'are not troubled by ambiguity and are enticed by complexity' (Belenky *et al.*, 1986: 139). Women constructivists develop connected knowing so that it is 'not simply an "objective" procedure but a way of weaving their passions and intellectual life into some recognizable whole' (Belenky *et al.*, 1986: 141); they 'establish a communion with what they are trying to understand' (Belenky *et al.*, 1986: 143). A central method is 'real talk', which includes discourse and exploration, talking and listening, questions, argument, speculation, and sharing, but in which domination is replaced by reciprocity and cooperation. Though idealists, constructivist women 'learn to live with compromise and to soften ideals which they find unworkable' (Belenky *et al.*, 1986: 152). They speak of 'integrating feeling and care into their work' (Belenky *et al.*, 1986: 152), and most strongly of a 'desire to have a "room of their own"... in a family and community and world that they helped make liveable' (Belenky *et al.*, 1986: 152).

What does this tell us about learning? Belenky and her colleagues offer us a typology of how women learn – and more broadly how they relate to knowledge. Their conclusions are of course limited to the women they studied. They emphasize the role of relationships, and the intimate relationship between the self, the mind and how people communicate with one other through talk. They suggest that the role of relationships, intimacy and communicative talk is more important among women than among men – or at least, that the ways in which communication takes place among men tends to differ in various ways. However, theirs is not fundamentally a comparative theory: they draw conclusions about women's learning, but they conduct no directly comparable research on men.

But of course they say something more than this. They speak of women's ways of knowing, not women's ways of learning. In other words, the way in which women relate to one another is not just a way of discovering about an objective world. They argue that knowledge is created in relationships between the 'knower', other 'knowers' and the material world.

Do Chinese learners learn differently?

One of the criticisms which Gilligan and others make of the developmental psychology literature is that it draws universal conclusions from studies based exclusively, or predominantly, on males. But they would themselves be open to a similar criticism: they draw universal conclusions about women from research based on women in the USA. In fact, the great bulk of the literature on how people learn is based on research conducted in the West (chiefly North America and Europe). The most significant attempt to address this weakness is by a number of educationalists and psychologists working in South East Asia, who have collaborated on a recent book (Watkins and Biggs, 1996).

The starting point for their research is described by John Biggs, a leading Australian constructivist educational psychologist who in 1987 took up the Chair of Education at the University of Hong Kong. He was struck by an apparent paradox. He knew that, as a result of modern research, there was fairly widespread agreement about what educational conditions encourage good learning. Effective learning is likely to take place in teaching environments with the following characteristics (Biggs, 1996a: 45–6).

- Teaching methods are varied, emphasizing student activity, self-regulation and student-centredness, with much cooperative and other group work.
- Content is presented in a meaningful context.
- Classes are small.
- Classroom climate is warm.
- High cognitive level outcomes are expected and addressed in assessment.
- Assessment is classroom-based and conducted in a non-threatening atmosphere.

On this basis, many East Asian educational systems must be producing low-quality learning. Westerners who teach students from societies such as Singapore, Malaysia, Hong Kong, China, Taiwan and other 'Confucian-Heritage Cultures' (CHCs) frequently comment that they prefer didactic teaching and rote learning to critical thinking, and treat their teacher as an unchallengeable authority. This applies whether the students are studying in East Asia or in the West. In East Asian countries, classes are normally large (typically well over 40). Teachers lecture a lot, and focus closely on getting the best results in externally set examinations. Examinations tend to focus on lower-level cognitive goals, are highly competitive, and put intense pressures on students and teachers alike. Expenditure on education has been much lower per capita than in the West (even in such affluent countries as Singapore and Hong Kong), and resources and support services, such as counselling, are poorer (Biggs, 1996a: 46–7).

At the same time, students from CHCs achieve far more than their Western counterparts. For example, overseas higher education students from CHCs studying in the USA perform much better than their IQ levels would predict. In their own countries, CHC school students' performances have been consistently better than Western nations'. For example, in a computational test at grade 5, only 1.4 per cent of Beijing students scored as low as the mean of corresponding US students. Such outcomes, Biggs felt, could not be achieved through rote learning.

Starting from these apparent paradoxes, Biggs and a number of his colleagues have investigated in detail how CHC students study and learn. Their findings (in research programmes still very much in progress) can be summarized as follows.

- Westerners' images of how Chinese students learn are based on Western preconceptions, and misjudge Chinese realities. For example, Gardner (1989) found that very young Chinese children have artistic skills well in advance of Americans of the same age, but they draw only from a few set models. Was this just imitation? What about creativity? He argued that the differences lay in beliefs about how various learning-related activities should be sequenced. Typically, Westerners believe exploration should precede the development of skill. Chinese educators in contrast believe skills should be developed first (which requires repetitive learning); this provides a basis to be creative with.
- There is an important distinction between 'rote learning' – mechanistic and without thought – and learning which uses repetition as a strategy to ensure accurate recall. If learning aims at understanding, and repetition is a means to this, it can be a strategy for deep rather than surface learning. It is a mistake to assume that all use of repetition in learning is a 'surface' approach: the key is in the context of the technique, rather than the specific technique itself.
- Westerners who teach Chinese students are often disappointed by the apparent unwillingness to respond to questions or enter discussion. But the numbers of students who seek one-to-one interaction with the teacher immediately after class, and who interact with other students, is probably higher than among comparable western students. (Chinese teachers typically have much lighter teaching timetables, to allow for interaction with students outside class.)
- While Western students tend to attribute success and failure to ability or the lack of it, CHC students see effort or lack of effort as the primary factor. For instance, Hau and Salili (1991) show that Hong Kong secondary-school students attribute success to (in order): effort, interest in study, study skill, mood and only then ability. This is a complex phenomenon,

grounded in a web of different factors, but does mean that CHC students tend to spend more 'time on task' in any period of study, and more time in studying outside the class.

- Although CHC students respond relatively poorly to teacher-led discussion in class, they collaborate spontaneously in handling unfamiliar situations, such as a new assessment task. Tang (1996) found 87 per cent of her sample of Hong Kong university students engaged in collaborative learning without any suggestion from their teachers.

Behind these findings lies a more significant conclusion. How Chinese students learn is intimately linked to the nature of Chinese culture and society. Confucian thought emphasizes that all people are educable and perfectable. Chinese society is characterized by collectivism and 'filial piety' – loyalty and obedience within a family context. Individuals' identities are formed within this family, collective, context, and they identify strongly with social and work groups. An example of how important this is can be found in Salili's comparison of how British and Chinese secondary-school students think about achievement. The Chinese saw success in academic work and career as very closely related to success in family and social life; for the British, these two areas of achievement were unrelated (Salili, 1996).

Conclusion

While the processes of learning are universal, what we learn and the ways in which we learn are strongly influenced by social characteristics such as gender and ethnicity. In the remaining chapters of this book, we examine some of the ways and contexts in which opportunities for learning are presented, and in which learning occurs.

Chapter 9

Self-directed learning

Although culture and social context form the context for learning, and strongly influence the processes involved, in a very important sense all learning remains individual. For, despite talk about the 'learning society' and the 'learning organization', logically (and psychologically) only individuals can learn. Learning is generally taken to entail some kind of internalizing of that which is 'learnt', and this in turn can only be directly experienced by individuals.

In most societies schooling is now universal and compulsory, but in recent years 'consumer sovereignty' has been all the rage. Social forces are propelling all forms of education towards individualized modes of learning. In schools and further and higher education, for instance, modularization and workplace learning projects are symptoms of the powerful trend towards individualizing learning, as are the reflective learning processes now almost universal in professional education and training. In every sector of education, training and development, the 'curriculum' is being replaced by individualized or 'customized' learning programmes. These are designed to suit the learner, the employer, the industry, profession or even the state itself.

Adult education, however, has always embraced the principle of individualized learning. Adult education has never been compulsory or universal, and has never been organized according to traditional curriculum principles, but rather as individualized learning programmes. It also implies that teachers must accept that adults can and do learn without the help of teachers. A role of adult educators is to facilitate self-directed, reflective and critical learning on the part of individual learners.

In its principles and practice, liberal adult education has always reflected a concept of adulthood which stressed individualism and autonomy. From this comes a focus on such concepts as self-determination, self-actualization or self-transformation as the underlying philosophy of all education for adults.

In terms of educational practice, this has entailed a view of adult learning as essentially self-planned or self-directed. This means that all learning is individual. Educationally, it also means that individual learners should have control of – should be able to plan or direct – their own learning. As a result, adult educators have usually taken an enabling or facilitating role towards learners, rather than one based upon pedagogic principles of instruction.

Based on this philosophy, an extensive literature on the subject of self-directed learning has developed, reflecting research, theory and practice. In this chapter we consider the contributions of four major theorists who have established self-directed learning as a fundamental principle of adult education: Cyril Houle, Allen Tough, Malcolm Knowles and Stephen Brookfield.

Cyril Houle

Adult educators' concern with self-directed learning originated in the writings of several North American scholars in the 1960s. Of these, perhaps the most influential was Cyril Houle's book *The Inquiring Mind* (1961). Adult educators have always had a particular interest in learners' motivation. Unlike schools and further and higher education, adult education is voluntary rather than compulsory. In this spirit, Houle identified three broad categories of learner 'orientations' to study.

- *Goal-oriented*. For these learners, motivation was instrumental, the means to some end, such as their career.
- *Activity-oriented*. For these learners, motivation was the social activities and interaction which learning may offer.
- *Learning-oriented*. For these learners, motivation was intrinsic and learning was simply undertaken for its own sake. (Houle, 1961: 15–16)

Later researchers constructed more sophisticated typologies. But Houle had drawn attention to the fact that many adult learners were self-motivated in their learning. This carried implications for concepts such as personal growth and development.

Houle's work stimulated a great deal of research. He himself developed his analysis of the educational frameworks in which adult learners' needs might be met. In *The Design of Education* (1972) he proposed eleven categories of 'educational situations'. The first was independent study. Here he set out fundamental principles of self-directed learning, and proposed how it could be researched.

> Since independent study is, by definition, a wholly self-guided way of designing and controlling an educational activity, it can be examined in depth only by one who analyzes his own experience or that reported to him. (Houle 1972: 91)

It follows from this that the only knowledge we could have of this kind of learning is anecdotal, 'drawn from the biographies or autobiographies of distinguished men and women'. In a later work, *Patterns of Learning* (1984), Houle followed up this insight into what he called 'life-span learning'. He looked at the lives and work of historical figures such as Montaigne, Thoreau and Billy Graham, in order to construct a portrait of the lifelong self-directed learner. But these are comparatively well-known people. As Houle says:

> Little is known about the nature or frequency of independent study in the lives of the undistinguished individuals who make up the great majority of mankind. (Houle 1972: 92)

However, evidence was emerging that ordinary people did, in fact, engage in systematic and purposeful independent study. Citing research carried out by Johnstone and Rivera (1965), Houle referred to the nearly nine million Americans who were engaged in some kind of independent learning activity. He began to analyse what this particular 'educational situation' meant, and what orientations and strategies the learners who took this difficult road adopted. 'Almost at once,' he says, 'most of them begin to feel inadequate.' The implications for the educator are clear:

> An independent study situation is, in the deepest sense, a cooperative art in which learning must be guided at every point by the distinctive individualism of the learner. He must design and conduct his program with the realization that it is based on his own uniqueness, that it has meaning only as it changes him, and that at every point he must be its master. (Houle, 1972: 96)

Houle also referred to Allen Tough's research into what he called 'self-planned learning'. This was to prove highly influential in the development of the theory and practice of self-directed learning.

Allen Tough

Tough's survey was carried out in 1970 at the Ontario Institute for Studies in Education in Canada. It was an attempt to improve on the anecdotal evidence of self-directed learning amongst the ordinary people to which Houle referred. Tough carried out interview-based research into samples of people from various occupational and other social groups. These were blue-collar workers, men and women in low status white-collar jobs, elementary school teachers, municipal politicians, social science professors, and upper-middle-class women with preschool children.

The central focus of Tough's research was called the 'learning project'. He defined this in quantified terms as 'a series of related episodes, adding up to at least seven hours':

> In each episode, more than half of the person's total motivation is to gain and retain certain fairly clear knowledge and skill, or to produce some other lasting change in himself. (Tough, 1979: 6)

On this research basis, Tough found that :

> The typical person conducts about eight learning projects in one year... All but one of the 66 interviewees had conducted at least one learning project in the past year, which produces an astounding 'participation rate' of 98 per cent. (Tough, 1979: 17)

Tough's 'learning projects' have subsequently proved very important in the development of the concept of self-directed learning. This is because Tough drew attention, for the first time and in a systematic way, to how much people engage in purposeful study, and the range of their reasons. The sheer volume of learning undertaken in this way was remarkable. On average, his interviewees spent 'about 700 or 800 hours a year' engaged in various learning projects, and 'roughly 90 hours' on each one (Tough, 1979: 18). Very little of this was for formal credit. Most of it fell into Houle's third category of orientations to study, namely, 'learning-oriented' or undertaken for their own sake:

> Despite the detailed questions and the subsequent probing, we found that only 0.7 per cent of all the learning projects were for credit. Apparently learning for credit forms only a small portion of all adult learning. (Tough, 1979: 19)

What was much more universal was the degree of motivation and persistence which the learners displayed in pursuit of their learning projects:

> Many unsolicited statements and actions during interviews that convey enthusiasm and commitment confirm the quantitative data about the importance of learning projects. A strong determination to succeed, and perseverance despite difficulties, also indicate that many learning projects are very important to the person. (Tough, 1979: 19)

Tough's research into learning projects for personal growth and social change has been extremely significant in the long-term development of the theory, research and practice of self-directed learning. It has also been of lasting significance in adult education, as later commentators have confirmed:

> With the publication of *The Adult's Learning Projects* in 1971, numerous researchers began to adopt the methodology used by Tough in conducting additional studies with different segments of the adult population... In reviewing these replications, it should be noted that despite considerable variation in both the total number of learning projects and in the total percentage of self-planned projects, the findings from the original Tough investigation are largely substantiated. (Brockett and Hiemstra, 1991: 44)

Malcolm Knowles

Malcolm Knowles, like Tough, made a huge contribution to the development of adult learning theory and practice. Not so research-oriented, Knowles was much more concerned with what self-directed learning implied for teachers and learners, and for the theory of adult education and lifelong learning. We see in this section how he extended the concept of the learning project to constitute a general theory of learning.

At the same time as Houle and Tough's research became influential among adult educators in the United States, Knowles (1975) produced a practical handbook on self-directed learning, designed to be used by both learners and teachers. It was in three parts, concerned respectively with the learner, the teacher and the learning resources. The first of these took the implications of Tough's research and developed them into a general theory of education, effectively presenting a philosophy of self-directed learning in the context of personal growth, social change and lifelong learning.

The first part of Knowles' book consists basically of four 'inquiry projects'. His general theory of self-directed learning may be derived from these. They anticipate many aspects of the move away from education towards lifelong learning, which were outlined in chapters 1 and 2 of this book.

In the first inquiry project, Knowles addresses the question 'Why self-directed learning?' He provides three immediate answers to this question.

- Self-directed learners are better learners: 'people who take the initiative in learning... learn more things, and learn better, than do people who sit at the feet of teachers passively waiting to be taught.'
- Adults do not need teachers, in the sense that they are perfectly capable of taking charge of their own learning. Therefore, 'self-directed learning is more in tune with our natural processes of psychological development'.
- The de-institutionalization of education, in the form of open and independent learning systems, is creating a need for learners to develop appropriate skills. 'Students entering into these programs without having learned the skills of self-directed inquiry will experience anxiety, frustration and often failure, and so will their teachers.' (Knowles, 1975: 14–15)

Apart from these immediate reasons for adopting self-directed learning, however, there are other reasons which Knowles described in terms not unlike those used more recently to describe the passing of the 'modern' era:

> The simple truth is that we are entering into a strange new world in which rapid change will be the only stable characteristic and this simple truth has several radical implications for education and learning. (Knowles, 1975: 15)

The three radical implications which Knowles drew are as follows:

- The growth of knowledge itself means that we need to learn in very different ways: 'it is no longer realistic to define the purpose of education as transmitting what is known.' The skills of self-directed learning are therefore necessary for everyone to develop throughout their lifetime.
- Learning must be experiential. Instead of thinking about learning as 'what is taught', we must learn from everything we do: 'we must exploit every experience as a "learning experience". Every institution in our community... becomes a resource for learning... Learning means making use of every resource – in or out of educational institutions – for our personal growth and development.'
- Learning can no longer be identified with schooling or initial education: 'it is no longer appropriate to equate education with youth... Education – or, even better, learning – must now be defined as a lifelong process.' (Knowles, 1975: 15–16)

He summed up these points by saying that:

> The 'why' of self-directed learning is survival – your own survival as an individual, and also the survival of the human race. Clearly, we are not talking here about something that would be nice or desirable; neither are we talking about some new educational fad. We are talking about a basic human competence – the ability to learn on one's own – that has suddenly become a prerequisite for living in this new world. (Knowles, 1975: 16–17)

In the second inquiry project, Knowles addressed the question 'What is self-directed learning?' He provides his own definition:

> In its broadest meaning, 'self-directed learning' describes a process in which individuals take the initiative, with or without the help of others, in diagnosing their learning needs, formulating learning goals, identifying human and material resources for learning, choosing and implementing appropriate learning strategies, and evaluating learning outcomes. (Knowles, 1975: 18)

He insisted that, although there had been many other names for this process – 'inquiry method', 'independent learning', 'self-instruction' and so on – most of these implied learning 'in isolation'. Self-directed learning, on the other hand, was usually a cooperative exercise: 'there is a lot of mutuality among a group of self-directed learners'. This led Knowles to a brief description of his idea of andragogy, or theory of adult learning, which he contrasts with pedagogy (concerned with the teaching of children). He was to develop this theory – for which he is best remembered – elsewhere. At this point, it is sufficient to say that in Knowles' view adult learning, unlike that of children, is characteristically self-directed.

In his third inquiry project, Knowles addressed the question 'What competencies are required for self-directed learning?' The fourth project is 'Designing a learning plan'. This last takes the form of a learning contract, a form of learning we shall describe in the next chapter of this book.

Nearly a quarter of a century ago, therefore, Malcolm Knowles' concept of self-directed learning anticipated many of the developments now included in the term lifelong learning. The rest of Knowles' book was concerned with the implications of self-directed learning for the teacher, and with the learning resources needed to achieve it. Both are of major educational significance and have been much developed since he wrote. Thus, concepts such as andragogy, the learning contract and the idea of the teacher as facilitator have become part of the familiar language of education.

Since Knowles first propagated these ideas, other writers have taken them further. One of the most important is Stephen Brookfield, who developed the concept of self-directed learning into one of critical reflection or critical thinking as a logical consequence of this view of adult learning. It is to his writings we now turn.

Stephen Brookfield

The connection between self-directed learning and personal change has long been recognized. Allen Tough himself carried forward his research by examining how people change as a result of engaging in learning projects (Tough, 1982). Stephen Brookfield put self-directed learning at the heart of his own very influential theory of adult learning, but has been quite critical of the research tradition which Tough represents. Brookfield's criticisms question both its methodology and its implications. In a critical review of the research, he attempts to put self-directed learning into a quite different perspective. Acknowledging the powerful influence of the tradition, he argues that:

> As a result, we are in danger of accepting uncritically a new academic orthodoxy in adult education. Put simply, it is not uncommon to hear practitioners and theorists declaring as self-evident a number of doubtful propositions that make self-directed learning the goal and method of adult education. We repeatedly encounter the claim that adults are self-directed. This claim is often speedily followed by the self-contradictory proposition that continuing education should therefore be concerned with developing adults' powers of self-direction. (Brookfield, 1985: 5–6)

One of Brookfield's most important criticisms is that the concept of self-direction has been divorced from the social context or setting in which learning takes place. In his own research, he says:

> Despite these dimensions of independence, the learning activities of the adults whom I interviewed were placed consciously and deliberately within the context of informal learning networks. (Brookfield, 1985: 8)

In order to understand the concept of autonomy, Brookfield argues, individual learners need to examine their own perceptions of the social world. This is because these perceptions condition the choices they can make, and limit the extent of their real autonomy as members of society. Only when learners begin to think critically about the social world, and about their capacity to shape it to their own needs rather than being conditioned by it, can they be really autonomous and self-directed. Brookfield rejects the 'technicist' perspective on self-directed learning, which is concerned only with ways in which learners can plan their own learning, access their own resources and achieve their aims. Brookfield's theory is concerned with critical reflection and personal meaning. This is the true perspective which educators should recognize:

> When the techniques of self-directed learning are allied with the adult's quest for critical reflection and the creation of personal meaning after due consideration of a range of alternative value frameworks and action possibilities, then the most complete form of self-directed learning is exemplified. This most fully adult form of self-directed learning is one in which critical reflection on the contextual and contingent aspects of reality, the exploration of alternative perspectives and meaning systems, and the alteration of personal and social circumstances are all present. (Brookfield, 1985: 15)

Brookfield, then, wants to take the theory of self-directed learning much further than Tough's ideas about individual change. He tries to move it towards a position of critical thinking about society and the individual's place in it. In this way, he argues, it becomes much more manifestly concerned with social change.

Brookfield was also critical of the methodology of self-directed learning research. He argued that its samples of respondents are unrepresentative in terms of a range of important class and cultural variables. It employed 'quasi-quantitative' instruments, which did not capture the real value of individual learning activities. Such criticisms have not been universally accepted. Brookfield and others, for instance, are said to 'convey an inaccurate picture of the characteristics of the self-directed learning research' (Long *et al.*, 1992: 5). The consensus remains that the research tradition that stimulated Tough and others is valid, and represents a major contribution to our understanding of how adults learn.

Nevertheless, Brookfield has developed out of the idea of self-directed learning a highly influential theory about the nature and purpose of adult education. He has subsequently worked out in detail his view of critical thinking, and of ways of 'challenging adults to explore alternative ways of thinking and acting' (Brookfield, 1987).

In the hands of writers such as Brookfield learning is wholly identified with personal growth and social change. We have therefore come a long way from the initial conception of self-directed learning as an entirely individualized expression of how people learn.

From theory to practice

The theorists whose work we have summarized have all developed their ideas from a concept of self-directed learning.

- *Cyril Houle* developed the concept of independent study on the part of learning-orientated adults. He drew attention to the considerable number of people whose motivation to learn is intrinsic, and who learn for reasons of personal growth and development.
- *Allen Tough* developed the concept of the adult learning project, with research which drew attention to the ways in which adults learn independently of teachers and formal educational institutions.
- *Malcolm Knowles* developed the concept of andragogy as a general theory of adult learning and adult education, distinguishing this very sharply from the pedagogy which is associated with the education of children.
- *Stephen Brookfield* developed a concept of critical thinking. This takes genuine self-directed learning to be inseparable from learning how to achieve a sense of personal meaning in the face of social and cultural pressures to conform to the status quo.

These theorists have also explored some of the consequences of their concepts of self-directed learning for educational practice, to which we finally turn.

In considering the implications of his own theory of self-planned learning and major personal change, Allen Tough offered five answers to the question of how this might be facilitated.

- The first is, in effect, staff development. 'I think probably the largest change in our institutions will come from learning how to facilitate the learning of the staffs of those institutions.' In other words, it is only possible to facilitate the learning of others if you know how to facilitate your own.
- 'Major personal change' needs to be integrated into the curriculum itself. Instead of being merely an indirect intention of the education process, it needs to be incorporated as an actual aim.
- The formal education system needs to be supplemented by informal networks of learning, such as skill exchanges, 'peer matching services' and 'directories of freelancers'.

- The range of choice and support for students in formal systems needs to be increased, especially in terms of teaching methods and the content of learning.
- The emphasis on credit needs to be decreased. Tough's own research demonstrated that only a small number of adults want to undertake their learning projects for accreditation purposes. (Tough, 1993: 39–41)

Since the 1970s, when Tough was developing his theories, some of these implications for practice have become the orthodoxy of lifelong learning. One of the most important concepts to be developed is that of the teacher as facilitator. Some of the most significant practical implications of self-directed learning theory therefore concern changes in educational roles.

Here is a typical list of the specific roles which are needed in order to promote self-direction in learning:

- provide information on certain topics through lecturing and the use of media or other learning techniques;
- serve as a resource for an individual or for a small group on certain portions of the learning content;
- assist learners to assess their needs and competencies so each person can map out an individual learning path;
- provide feedback on successive drafts of each person's learning plan or contract;
- locate available resources or secure new information on topics identified through needs assessment;
- build a resource collection of information, media and models related to a variety of topics or areas of study;
- arrange for contacts with resource people on special topics and set up learning experiences for individuals and small groups beyond normal large group sessions;
- work with learners outside formal or group settings as a stimulator or sounding board;
- help learners develop an attitude about and approach to learning that fosters independence;
- promote discussion, raising of questions and small-group activity to stimulate interest in the learning experience;
- help develop a positive attitude toward learning and self-directed inquiry;
- manage a learning process that includes such activities as continuous diagnosis of needs, acquisition of continuous feedback and fostering of learner involvement;
- serve as a validator or evaluator of learner accomplishment both throughout and at the end of a learning experience. (Brockett and Hiemstra, 1991: 108–109)

These implications for the role of facilitator of self-directed learning can be related to the general theories of learning outlined above. The same authors had earlier developed their account of bridging the theory–practice gap in four areas.

- Learners' self-directedness needs to be viewed as a continuum, and not an 'all-or-nothing concept'. Diversity of learning styles means that attention must be paid to the fact that 'individuals vary in their readiness for self-direction'.
- The role of facilitation: developing teaching strategies, reconceptualizing the role of instructor and devising 'tools for self-directed learning', such as learning contracts and written learning materials.
- The development of policies for learners, educators and institutions, in order to promote self-directed learning.
- There are ethical issues to address, such as the relationship between the learner and the facilitator, and institutional issues such as quality and standards of academic achievement. (Brockett and Hiemstra, 1985)

Conclusion

This chapter has introduced some of the contributions to the theory of self-directed learning. We have reviewed some of the practical implications of this particular view of the learning process for educators and educational institutions. The work of Houle, Tough, Knowles and Brookfield has resulted in wider conceptions of learning, especially in relation to personal growth and social change. What began as a rather individualistic view of learning has, over the years, developed into a much broader conception. For example, there is now an annual international conference on self-directed learning in which industry and commerce, as well as academics, participate. The broader approach to self-directed learning which has evolved is consistent with the idea of lifelong learning itself.

Chapter 10

Contracts and learning

Over the past two decades or so, the idea that contracts have a role in learning has become popular. There are a number of reasons for this. Explaining the relationship between contracts and learning is therefore not straightforward. This chapter explains the background to the interest in contracts. This is partly a matter of the social context of learning, but as with other recent developments in learning theory, it also relates to general developments in the social and political organization of modern states.

We begin by looking briefly at the background to contracts and their social role. We then discuss the role of contracts in education and training. There are several aspects to this. First, we examine the idea of learning contracts. We look at the relationship between learning contracts and the notion of competence. We then discuss the idea that we now live in a 'contracting society'. One of the ways in which educational institutions have made use of learning contracts is in connection with modularization. Next we discuss issues relating to language and social power in the negotiation of contracts. In the concluding section, we raise again the open question as to whether the use of contracts increases or reduces freedom and autonomy in learning.

The search for predictability

Human learning is a wondrous phenomenon. We all do it. Very often, though not always, we know when we have learnt something. But we can hardly know exactly what we are going to learn! Learning always has this vital dimension of creativity and unpredictability. When we start to learn something, we never know exactly where the process will take us. This makes learning exciting, innovative and valuable – yet at the same time challenging, risky and potentially threatening. Learning can threaten our own established ideas and understandings. And what is true for individuals is also true for groups, organizations and societies. They need to learn, but learning can also threaten them.

As a result, societies and organizations – or more accurately, the powerful people within them – have always looked for ways of controlling what people learn. If they cannot control what is learnt, they try at least to make the learning and its effects more predictable. So too with individuals. We may want a training course to teach us something new, but we generally want some idea beforehand of the kind of experience we shall be having.

One of the main ways in which societies, organizations and individuals have achieved this predictability in learning over recent centuries has been through education. People have not learnt at random: what they have learnt has been structured through systems of schools, universities, curricula, teachers, examinations and so forth. Of course, even with a set curriculum we never know exactly what someone will learn when they study. Learning is always in that sense unique. But for most people, the education system provides a remarkable degree of uniformity of experience and learning.

But as we have seen, learning is not confined to the formal education system. People learn throughout their lives. They learn in and from the social situations which they experience. Where social structures are relatively stable, there is a good measure of predictability in what people learn. Throughout the twentieth century, for example, British working-class males have developed extensive knowledge of soccer. This is a vast and ever-changing field, requiring constant updating of technical and social knowledge. Yet the fact that it is constantly changing does not prevent it being highly predictable and stable. Rarely indeed has knowledge of football threatened the social order! Even the informal and incidental learning which takes place at work becomes largely predictable when the workplace itself is ordered and relatively unchanging.

Yet one of the messages of this book has been the increasingly unstable and risky nature of our social experience. The world changes, and changes ever faster. Social structures – where people live, who they live with, what they do in their leisure time and with whom – can no longer be taken for granted. Structures of work organization are no longer set for long periods. In these circumstances, systems of educational provision and other established approaches to the provision of learning no longer seem adequate. What we need to learn changes so quickly that what formal systems offer is no longer relevant.

In these circumstances, the idea of the contract has become popular. Contracts, with their implication of agreement between two parties, seem to provide a mechanism for introducing a measure of order and predictability. All around us the world may be changing; but if I agree to teach you something, this contract between us provides a measure of mutual certainty. What is more, the fact that we have both agreed suggests that we are both happy with the arrangement.

Contracts and markets

One reason why late modern or postmodern societies are unpredictable and risky is that they are increasingly organized on a market basis. In economic terms, markets are based on contracts between buyer and sellers for the provision of goods or services. The simplicity of the contractual relationship stems from the fact that the parties specify precisely the terms of the transaction: 'Apples: 50 pence a pound!'

In fact, of course, markets and contracts are not that simple. Even in the street-corner fruit and vegetable market, I rely on the fact that when I hand over my 50 pence, the seller will give me the full pound of apples he has promised and that they will be as fresh as the ones on show. All contracts call for a degree of trust between the parties. In more complex transactions, a large measure of trust may be called for. This trust is not created by the contract: the contract only works because the trust exists. (Of course, the successful completion of one contract helps build trust between buyer and seller.)

Contracts, therefore, have a deceptive simplicity. They appear to be agreements between two parties, but in fact they work because the two parties are surrounded by a complex network of social arrangements. These enable the parties to trust one another. This may be because of strong personal trust, but it can also be because a professional or legal framework exists.

Contracts provide a mechanism of establishing a firm relationship between two parties. This is one reason why they are increasingly popular in a world of change. They provide a point of stability. But in the world of learning, education and training, interest in contracts comes in several forms. Each perspective on contracts has its own specific characteristics. It is to these that we now turn.

Learning contracts: self-direction and personal autonomy

The first, and in many ways the most attractive, attempt to bring the language of contracts into the practice of learning comes from North American self-directed learning (see also chapter 9). Brockett and Hiemstra assert (1991: 223) that there is a 'continuing need to promote the use of learning contracts' to encourage self-directed learning. On this argument, the learning contract provides the learner with a key to the learning process. Through the learning contract, learners can diagnose their own learning needs, plan and schedule their own learning activities, work out the resources they will need, and evaluate the outcomes of their experience. It is, as Brookfield (1986: 81) points out, the 'chief mechanism' used by advocates of self-directed learning, and has been applied in adult education, higher education, professional education, training and religious education.

The origins of this perspective on learning contracts lie in the work of the US adult educator Malcolm Knowles, and his notion of andragogy. As individuals mature, Knowles (1980: 44–5) argued, they move from being 'a dependent personality toward being a self-directed human being'. They also seek to learn in relation to their roles in society, and they seek knowledge which can be applied rapidly, rather than stored for possible later use. This meant that the notion of curriculum was an inappropriate one for the education of adults. The way to organize adult learning was not by subject but by problem area. Indeed, he recommended the replacement of the term 'curriculum' by 'programme'.

One central implication of Knowles' andragogical approach, however, related to the process of programme planning. As 'self-directed human beings', learners should be involved in planning their own learning. The teacher was only 'a procedural guide and content resource' (Knowles, 1980: 48) – a facilitator. The planning of learning was a mutual responsibility for teacher and learner.

The mechanics of this mutual planning process could, however, be rather complex. Knowles argued that where there were fewer than about thirty students, they could be directly involved in planning. Beyond this size, various committees, teams and other mechanisms would be needed to ensure that learners were properly involved in the planning. But these large-scale negotiations are inevitably relatively bureaucratized activities. Students can rapidly lose a genuine sense of 'ownership' over the resultant programme design.

It was research on individual learning in the 1960s and 1970s which provided the basis for the development of the idea of the learning contract (Knowles, 1986: 27; 40–41). In adult education, negotiation had tended to be seen as a collective exercise: a negotiation between a group of students and their teacher. When Allen Tough (1979) showed that individual learners engaged in serious learning projects, it was clear that individuals could also take part in negotiations about what they should learn. The problem was just technical. Knowles labelled the agreements which resulted from these negotiations 'learning contracts'. He maintained that the learning contract should be a written document; he provides (1986) a template and some examples.

How were learning contracts to be negotiated? Knowles played a major role in popularizing the idea, and drew heavily on his earlier work in suggesting how they should be developed. Making a learning contract involves much the same steps as planning any educational or training programme. The chief difference is that the planning is done by the learner (or, commonly, by the learner in discussion with a facilitator of some kind). Knowles (1986: 27–32) recommends the following steps in developing a learning contract.

- Diagnose your learning needs.
- Specify your learning objectives.
- Specify learning resources and strategies.
- Specify evidence of accomplishment.
- Specify how the evidence will be validated.
- Review your contract with consultants.
- Carry out the contract.
- Evaluate your learning.

The similarity between these steps and Knowles' own formula for what educators should do in the programme-planning process is very close (see Knowles, 1980).

An example of developing a learning contract can be drawn from a postgraduate Masters degree for practitioners in the field of training and consultancy. On this course learning contracts are used extensively, particularly for the development of professional skills: contracts are negotiated with, and then assessed with, peers on the course. Thus one student identified a learning need in the area of assertiveness. She agreed with peers that she would collect evidence of several examples of her improved assertive behaviour. She drew on literature on assertiveness, and the help of a colleague who had attended an assertiveness training course, as resources in order to carry out the contract. She did this successfully according to the agreed aims and criteria.

During the 1980s and 1990s, learning contracts based roughly on Knowles' model have been implemented in a range of settings. According to their advocates (eg McAllister, 1996; Henfield and Waldron, 1988; Richardson, 1988), learning contracts have a number of advantages.

- They provide students with a greater sense of control over the learning process.
- They strengthen students' motivation to learn.
- They encourage deeper and more holistic (rather than surface) approaches to learning.
- They encourage self-assessment.
- They develop students' skills in planning their own learning, and encourage them to plan for future learning.

- In continuing education, they encourage practitioners to reflect on their current practice.
- They encourage cooperative and sharing approaches to learning.

Some negative experience has been reported. Henfield and Waldron (1988: 211) remark that negotiation of learning contracts is 'necessarily time-consuming for the individuals and course tutors'. McAllister (1996: 202–3) found that the format of learning contracts can confuse students, that some students did not know what their learning needs were, that learning contracts can trigger anxiety in some students, and that some students prefer teacher direction and dislike being expected to make decisions about their own learning. Students could also identify too many learning objectives. Counselling was vital to help them understand the complexity of the learning tasks and to set achievable goals. This finding has some similarities with Henfield and Waldron's conclusion (1988: 210) that some students may overestimate their capabilities at the outset.

Contracts and competence

Key elements of a learning contract, according to Knowles, are diagnosing your learning needs, specifying your learning objectives, and setting out what will count as evidence that these have been achieved. As we have seen, research shows that these are precisely the areas where problems arise. A lawyer might say that they are the difficulties of how to specify the terms of the learning contract. Given that, by definition, learners do not know what they have not yet learnt, how can they play an effective part in setting out learning objectives and planning how to get there? Doesn't this even make it rather difficult to state clearly what we do know?

This was one of the key problems which Knowles faced when developing his theory of andragogy. He solved it by drawing on the notion of competence. Competence is an idea drawn from behavioural approaches to psychology. It consists of describing the requirements of social roles in terms of observable behaviour. The work of a plumber, for example, is described in terms of specific skills involved in installing and mending pipes and so forth. The key is that specific skills are as far as possible separated out, so that a person can be observed to be capable of performing sub-task X but not sub-task Y. Other examples of competencies are: 'to type at 50 words per minute', 'to peel a potato', 'to keep the accounts of a small business'.

For Knowles, this provided the solution to the learning-contract conundrum. Learners were encouraged to describe in objective or behavioural terms what it is they wanted to be competent to do ('competences' or 'competencies'). As a learner, all I need to do is identify what I can do already, and compare it with the list of competencies which apply to the specific task. I am suddenly empowered: I can see exactly where I stand.

Of course, many competencies are in practice rather complex. Being able to manage a small business, for example, or to be a nurse or a plumber involve a vast range of competencies. Specifying them in detail is time-consuming. As Knowles (1980: 229) himself acknowledged, the tasks required to carry out most roles are constantly changing. It is therefore necessary continuously to review and update competence specifications. What is more, there are profound differences between specifying competence in skills and knowledge on the one hand, and in attitudes, interests and values on the other. Again, there are some technologies which help this process (eg Bloom, 1956), but profound problems remain. Can I really assess reliably, for instance, whether I have the right attitude and values to become a nurse or a plumber? Or, what attitudes and values I need?

The 'contracting society'

So far, we have discussed learning contracts as a technique whereby learners can work out learning plans appropriate to their own needs. Although learning contracts have often been used in this way, another rather more complex model of the learning contract has also emerged. This approach stems from a rather obvious feature of contracts, but one which was rather submerged in the early enthusiasm for learning contracts as empowering learners. Contracts are in fact the result of negotiation between two parties. Negotiations are not always between equals. While in some senses – the legal sense, and the sense that economists use, for example – both parties to a contract enter into it voluntarily, this does not mean that each gains as much or that each has as much influence on the terms of the contract.

This is an argument developed eloquently by Michael Collins. The rhetoric of learning contracts and self-directed learning, he says, encourages a 'misleading scenario' of adults 'voluntarily directing their educational projects through formal learning contracts'. In fact, Collins says, learning contracts and self-directed learning in institutional settings typically place

> the direction of their learning subtly, but firmly, in the hands of experts who serve predominantly institutionalized interests. Self-directed learning, systematically defined as it is in prevailing adult education practice, permits the learner to choose between options already defined by formal systems. (Collins, 1991: 24)

It is, of course, inevitably true that the options which learners have for learning are structured by the opportunities available. You can only enrol in a class on Anglo-Saxon jewellery if such a class is offered. If no class is available, of course, you can plan a self-study programme. Even for this, the effectiveness of your studies will be influenced by whether you have access to a good library, a museum with relevant exhibits, the Internet or a good bookshop (and a generous bank account!)

But it is not just that the framework within which learning contracts are negotiated is set by institutions. Increasingly, institutions have seen themselves as active negotiators in the formulation of learning contracts. This trend stems from a number of factors. Probably the strongest is the growth of what has been called a 'contracting society'. At all levels of society, from central government down, funds are now given only for the completion of very specific tasks. Even in the education sector, there are many examples. Until the 1980s, Britain's local education authorities maintained and funded further education colleges, but left them fairly free to decide on their policies. Now, the Further Education Funding Council specifies in detail what colleges should deliver in return for the funds it administers.

A contracting society also means, of course, the contraction of the amounts of public finance available. It is very much the ethos of efficiency and effectiveness: doing more for less. But part and parcel of this is also targeting: only using money for exactly what it was meant for. To many people this is a self-evident proposition: why should money, especially public money, be used for what it was not meant for? But it is important to recognize that it increases the pressures involved in the negotiating exercise. Very simply, institutions that are short of money are less able to accommodate the objectives of a diverse range of learners.

Governments have reduced the volume of funds they distribute. They now see their relationship with educational institutions much more as contracting for the provision of specific educational and training services. Other organizations have read the runes, and come to similar conclusions. Employers and professional bodies, in particular, have come to see the contract as a fulcrum for exercising leverage over the world of learning. The view that educational opportunities should be highly relevant to the needs of business and commerce has many powerful advocates, of course. Stephenson and Laycock (1993: 18), for example, argue that learning contracts enable employers to participate in developing student learning plans, plan more effective work placements, target student sponsorship more accurately, spot and recruit talent, and demonstrate to students that the programmes they are studying are relevant.

The extension of the language of contracts into education and training has other implications. Knowles spoke of learning contracts as relatively open and informal agreements between learner and mentor. In an educational market, learning contracts are no longer 'gentlemen's agreements'. Increasingly, they are contracts for educational services. Learners expect educational services to be provided in the same way as they expect a travel agent to organize the holiday they want or a plumber to fix their hot water. In this world, learning contracts become just another form of contract. Travel agents who organize bad holidays can expect legal action. Why should the same rules not apply to educational organizations which do not deliver the learning they promise?

The answer, of course, is that disappointed students are increasingly taking legal action against schools, colleges and universities. The areas of litigation are so far relatively limited, but education law is a growth area. Certainly, from a lawyer's point of view, learning contracts are a fascinating area. Malcolm Knowles, for example, suggests that we might contract not just to learn something, but to attain certain grades in an assessment. This would, after all, be an 'objective' way of discovering whether the contract had been fulfilled. But it raises the prospect of students taking legal action against tutors or colleges because, for example, they have only attained 45 per cent rather than the 65 per cent they were led to expect!

Learning contracts and modular learning

One of the ways institutions have attempted to harness the potential of the learning contract is through linking it with the idea of modularization. Modularization became popular in educational institutions in the late 1980s and early 1990s. Though there were some educational arguments, pressure to modularize was generally driven by cost and efficiency considerations. Educational institutions would offer a given range of modules. Learners – students – would negotiate a 'contract' with the institution to take a certain number (and perhaps a certain mix) of modules. Satisfactory completion would lead to a qualification of some kind.

Critics of this approach argued that it meant an erosion of the notion of a curriculum. Students were no longer to be guided through a range and hierarchy of knowledge in a certain logical sequence. Rather, they said, students would 'pick and mix' modules which might have little or no relevance to one another. This was, however, a situation where critics and advocates agreed on the facts. Supporters of modularization typically argued for it precisely on the ground that students should be treated as adult learners, capable of making informed decisions about their own learning needs. If they chose to 'pick and mix' modules which did not seem appropriate to the professors in one or another subject, that merely indicated that the logic and demands of subjects do not necessarily reflect the needs of individual learners.

The modularization debate is not one which we can explore in detail here, but certain aspects are worth noting. Ron Barnett (1997: 52) remarks that one of the unintended effects of modularization was the need to make each module 'transparent to largely uninformed customers'. If academic or educational choice is to be handed over to the student, then the student needs to be able to make (as consumer protection experts say) an informed choice. Yet we may think choosing what to learn is rather different from choosing what kind of butter to buy.

Barnett makes a second important observation. Introducing a learning-contract approach to programme delivery does not just mean more choice and more freedom for the learner. The freedom is constrained by the structures of the educational institution itself, as we have seen. But there is more. A learning contract approach brings major changes in the nature of educational organizations. One effect is that modular courses segment the student body. This can be alienating, making a sense of community far more difficult to build among the students of a course.

Traditionally, academic disciplines were reflected not only in the structure of the curriculum, but in departmental and organizational structures. Students were located within such departments. Now, with autonomous learners making choices about their studies, any link between them and a 'home' department or subject is largely accidental. With linked changes in accounting practices and so forth, much of the rationale for traditional educational and academic structures breaks down. In short, the institutions with which learners negotiate their contracts are no longer the same. In one way, of course, this is what many early advocates of learning contracts sought. Knowles, for instance, saw educational structures as in many respects oppressive, especially to adults. Learning contracts have transformed them. Whether in practice the concept has remained true to what its early advocates intended is, however, a matter for debate.

The language of contracts

Contracts are made within constraints set by institutions, but they are also made within socially set constraints. An important contribution from social work is relevant here. Over the past decade or so, the notion of contract has become more important in that field too. Corden and Preston-Shoot (1987) and Pratt (1985) argued that contracts can improve the quality of the relationship between social workers and clients, by making them more negotiable and less coercive. Rojek and Collins (1987) have pointed out that contracts are negotiated through the use of language. The balance of power between social worker and client is strongly influenced by the nature of the communication process which takes place between them.

Rodger (1991) argues that this has profound implications. There are important differences in language systems used by different social classes, ethnic groups and professional social workers. This means that the 'common meaning' which social workers and clients read into agreements or contracts about objectives and tasks is 'illusory'. Social workers and their clients each construct a meaning for the contract. These meanings are likely to be different, at least in a number of ways. Rodger (1991: 65) argues that 'the experience of poverty, racism and living with economic insecurity', among other factors, shape clients' perceptions and meanings. For example, key notions of everyday life – 'help', 'duty', 'responsibility' – are understood differently by different social groups. They are shaped and interpreted 'in accordance with varying material circumstances and human priorities'. And, as Rodger rightly points out, 'it is the negotiation of meaning between practitioner and client which must be the focus of our attention, not merely the words uttered' (Rodger, 1991: 66).

But Rodger develops another argument. Interestingly, he bases this on research which has been very influential in education: Basil Bernstein's theory of codes. For Bernstein (1971), codes are 'ways of seeing' – and simultaneously 'ways of not seeing'. Rodger argues that social workers can interpret their roles, their relationship with their clients and their social worker–client contracts in terms of either an 'appreciative' or a 'corrective' code. An appreciative code releases clients from 'overweening control'. It allows them 'to assert themselves and personalize or exteriorize their particular qualities in the way tasks are selected and undertaken'. Self reliance is generated through 'doing' (Rodger, 1991: 75). With a corrective code, on the other hand, 'the location of power to evaluate the client becomes more explicit in a contract'. Social control flows back to the social work professional who has the ultimate authority to assess progress.

What can we draw for the notion of 'learning contract' from this discussion of contracts in social work? As we have seen, contracts related to learning are drawn at a range of levels. Some are essentially institutional. Many – including most 'learning contracts' – involve individuals, at least in part. Typically, in a learning contract a learner engages with an individual or an institution (often an individual representing an institution) who is also in a relationship of power. Only rarely does the learner have the ultimate authority to assess progress. Rodger argues that contracts are only meaningful 'if they are struck within the core of the client's discourse and founded on the practitioner's understanding of the client's accounting system'. How a client makes sense of 'his or her real world' must be the starting point. A similar point is crucial in the striking of a learning contract. They are, perhaps, too often struck in terms of institutional understandings.

These considerations take us back to the concerns about the importance of culture in learning, discussed in chapter 8. People's knowledge, skills and attitudes are constructed in an engagement with their cultures. We may not know exactly what the impact of different cultural backgrounds will be. But we do know that they will have an impact on how people construct meanings of new situations and experiences. Negotiating a learning contract is a new experience for many people. How they handle the situation, how they will make sense of it and how empowered – or constrained – they are by it will vary. Rodger's argument is founded on the experience of social-work professionals. But it raises important ethical questions about how educational institutions, teachers and facilitators should conduct themselves when negotiating learning contracts.

Contracts and freedom

The notion of contract has, therefore, been imported into the practice of many educational institutions. Its importance is apparent. Contracts are the fulcrum of the market relationship, and learning is increasingly market-driven. Individuals choose freely to make choices. Such is the ideology. But while there is a sense – not least the legal sense – in which contracts must be entered into voluntarily, the choice is always made within a certain set of parameters.

Learning, as Roby Kidd (1973) pointed out, is a transaction. In this sense, thinking of learning in terms of contracts represents no major change. But there is an important difference between different kinds of transaction. Teaching which occurs where the 'rules' of the transaction are the web of formal and informal understandings involved in a notion like teacher professionalism is one thing. When learning contracts are negotiated in a competitive educational market, the rules are different. Market pressures sweep aside the informalities of professional groups and bureaucracies.

The key area of debate, therefore, is whether – on balance – contracts in the area of learning increase or limit freedom. As with many debates with strong political overtones, the jury is still out. It may well never deliver a verdict! Learning contracts provide learners with more opportunities to make decisions about their own learning. However, these choices are always constrained. The constraints emerge partly unintentionally. They arise from institutional structures, and (as Rodger shows) from the very language which we use. Some would argue, for instance, that written contracts are by their nature oppressive in a learning context. But many constraints are set consciously. Institutions, for instance, have come to see learning contracts as two-sided. If learners can negotiate, so can institutions. Professions too attempt to use contracts to apply pressure, to influence what is taught and how. In such negotiations, protagonists – major institutions and individuals – are not evenly matched.

Chapter 11

Open and distance learning

Open-learning and distance-learning systems have developed rapidly in recent years. They have been widely accepted as one of the most important examples of the evolution of lifelong learning from traditional forms of education. They incorporate many of the features of the concept of lifelong learning introduced in the first part of this book.

This chapter introduces some of the theories of open and distance learning. It looks critically at the issues surrounding these educational developments. And it describes examples of these modes of learning in practice.

Neither 'openness' nor 'distance' are concepts usually associated with traditional education systems, which tended to be compulsory, institutionalized and based on fairly rigid curriculum structures. Traditionally, education has been face-to-face and classroom based. There were of course exceptions, particularly in large countries such as Australia. In general, however, traditional education was a closed system of learning in many respects. We must be careful not to import value judgements here, though. There is no necessary connection between open and distance learning and good or effective learning. We shall find that arguments are still put forward in favour of traditional education, and that there are many critical perspectives on open and distance learning.

Traditional education and closed institutions

In what senses might we describe traditional education as 'closed'? Here are some examples:

- It was institutionally based, in schools, colleges, universities and so on. By definition an institution has some kind of boundary around it – you are

either inside the boundary or not. By including and excluding, institutions involve barriers and are in some sense closed to the outside world.
- These barriers take the form of administrative rules and regulations which govern the time and place where learning occurs – in timetables, academic terms and classrooms.
- Traditional education was organized around a closed curriculum, so the content of learning was divided rigidly into subjects, disciplines, knowledge, skills and so on.
- Traditionally too, educational institutions held a monopoly over the accreditation of learning. This meant that only learning acquired in institutions of education could count as 'real' and be universally accepted.

This paints a picture of traditional education as a rigid system. Compulsory classroom knowledge is acquired in formal conditions, and any knowledge acquired from other sources would not be recognized as 'education'. No doubt this picture is in some respects unfair. In reality, traditional education systems have proved an effective and satisfying source of learning for many individuals.

But these are examples of the sense in which traditional education is a 'closed' system of learning. So how 'open' could an institution be, while still remaining an institution of some kind? Ivan Illich (1971) argued for a wholly de-institutionalized education system, but few would regard this as anything except utopian. Considerable scope remains, however, for moving from a relatively closed towards a relatively open situation.

The model that comes to mind, in Britain at least, is that of the Open University. Since it received its charter in 1969, the British Open University has been emulated in many other countries, from Israel to Sri Lanka and from Tanzania to Korea.

It is significant, however, that it has been at this university level of the education system that openness has been embraced and distance learning systems put in place (Rumble and Harry, 1982). The reason for this is that mature or adult study (involving, as we shall see, a high level of independent learning) is a prerequisite for effective learning in an open institution. Thus, it is in the university sector that we can begin to define open learning institutions.

Defining open learning

Perhaps the best way to begin to define open learning is to contrast it with closed learning systems. Here is a recent approach which seems to take this into account.

> Open learning is an elusive term, meaning many different things to different people. In the most general sense, it is a relative term, referring to degrees of

> openness compared to some existing practice. Hence, an open admissions policy is one which places few or no restrictions on entry, in contrast to those applying strict selection criteria. (Paul, 1993: 114)

Paul sees the evolution of open learning in higher education as the result of many factors, such as expansion and democratization of the system, economic investment, and so on. Open learning, he argues, 'is merely one of the most recent manifestations of a gradual trend towards the democratization of education' (Paul, 1993: 114). He sets out the dimensions of openness as follows.

- *Accessibility.* This involves such things as: open admissions policies; acknowledgement of students' prior commitments in the timing of study programmes; facilities for distance learning; the financial advantages of combining study with work and family life; student support services for those returning to study; and provision for the socially disadvantaged or for those hitherto excluded from access to education.
- *Flexibility.* This involves: frequent admission periods, rather than fixed terms or semesters; self-pacing of study for students, rather than more rigid timing of assessment; and optional access to student support services.
- *Learner control over content and structure.* Individual students have the ability to negotiate their learning. This means in practice: some choice of delivery systems as most appropriate to the student's learning needs and styles; maximum choice in the matter of subjects for study, such as is typically ensured by a modular system; the widest possible system for the accreditation of learning, by way of experiential learning, credit transfer and so on. (Paul, 1993: 116–20)

These typical features of open learning coincide very closely with the concept of lifelong learning outlined in the first part of this book. Accessibility, flexibility and a high degree of learner control all reflect the trend towards mass education systems, de-institutionalization and consumer sovereignty which lifelong learning involves.

Paul describes these features as an 'ideal-type' construct of 'open learning'. His concern is to measure institutions, in this case open universities, against them. For example, the British Open University fulfils some of these conditions of 'openness', such as accessibility or pace of learning. In other respects, such as curriculum content or assessment, he finds it more like a traditional 'closed' institution. Certainly when we try to define open learning, it overlaps with several other terms, especially independent learning and distance education. We need, therefore, to look more closely at the relation between these terms. In recent years they have come to be used synonymously, but they need to be held separate for purposes of analysis.

Open learning and distance education

An important writer on distance education, Börje Holmberg, acknowledging that the distinction between open learning and distance education has become blurred, has put it like this:

> The adjective 'open' occurs frequently in connection with distance education, no doubt because of the strong influence of the British Open University and other distance-teaching organizations that have adopted practices corresponding to and names containing this adjective. In these names, 'open' originally referred to access and to the avoidance of certain restrictions; in itself it has nothing to do with distance education... (Holmberg, 1995: 4)

Distance learning refers to a 'mode of delivery'. Open learning refers to features in the structure of institutions, features contained in Paul's 'ideal-type' described above. On this basis, the distinction would appear to be quite clear. However, distance learning has often been thought of as a sub-category of open learning, even though in a strict sense it is not. Open learning is not necessarily distance learning, and distance education, as we have seen in the case of the British Open University, is not necessarily open in every respect.

These distinctions need not be pursued further. Suffice it to say that both open learning and distance education can be seen as characteristics of lifelong learning itself. Given the apparent vagueness of the concept, Holmberg himself takes a somewhat pragmatic view.

> Against this background it seems doubtful if open learning is really a helpful term... But perhaps its very vagueness makes it acceptable to common usage. Educators who find distance education a forbidding term may feel like replacing it by open learning. (Holmberg, 1995: 6)

This last point seems to support the idea that in 'postmodern' times the style of the message is more important than its content. Certainly, 'open' has a comforting ring which perhaps 'distance' lacks. Keegan (1990) proposed the following definition of distance education as most useful and corresponding to reality:

- the quasi-permanent separation of teacher and learner throughout the length of the learning process (this distinguishes it from conventional face-to-face education);
- the influence of an educational organization both in the planning and preparation of learning materials and in the provision of student support services (this distinguishes it from private study and teach-yourself programmes);
- the use of technical media – print, audio, video or computer – to unite teacher and learner and carry the content of the course;
- the provision of two-way communication so that the student may benefit

from or even initiate dialogue (this distinguishes it from other uses of technology in education);
- the quasi-permanent absence of the learning group throughout the length of the learning process so that people are usually taught as individuals and not in groups, with the possibility of occasional meetings for both didactic and socialization purposes. (Keegan, 1990: 44)

Theories of distance education

In this section, we consider the work of three writers who have contributed significantly to the theory of distance education: Otto Peters, Michael Moore and lastly Börje Holmberg, whose work has already been mentioned.

Otto Peters

In some ways the work of Otto Peters expresses the critical and negative responses which distance education has attracted. His theoretical model, as we shall see, seems to suggest that the production element in distance learning reduces education to a kind of industrial production process. Like others, he sees distance education as lacking the vital element of face-to-face interpersonal communication, as lacking the human dimension of group interaction, and even as alienating learners from teachers and each other.

From a lifelong learning perspective, one dimension in Peters' work should be noted. He associates distance education strongly with industrial or 'modern' society. Distance education for him is an 'industrialized' mode of education, a form of 'Fordist' mass production. Peters shows that distance education was made possible by the production system of industrial society, and the rapid postal and other forms of communication this created. Correspondence courses were, after all, the original form of distance education. But he goes further than this. He compares the process of preparing and disseminating distance learning materials to an assembly line. It is a mass production and consumption system, with a division of labour similar to that which evolved under industrial capitalism. Before the era of industrialism, education was a craft skill, with a human dimension. This, Peters suggests, is missing in distance education, and this is why so many teachers instinctively resist it. Referring to what he calls the 'industrialized form of instruction', Peters says that:

> Implicitly, it underlines the fact that distance study must be carefully preplanned, prepared and organized, and that there is a division of labour, a growing use of technical equipment to work with, and the necessity of formalized evaluations. People become aware that these and other features of distance study are structurally the same as those that can be found in an industrialized process. (Peters, 1993: 15–16)

In his 'industrial' theory of distance education, therefore, Peters expresses some of the reservations that teachers with a more 'traditional' approach to their work have often expressed. This debate has been continued however by Rumble (1995) who asks questions about the Fordist nature of production in the British Open University. However, many of the smaller providers have already moved into a smaller, arguably post-Fordist, mode of production. (Post-Fordism refers to flexible, tailor-made production for 'niche-markets'.)

It is precisely in the area of communications and media that postmodern society is most recognizable. Our next theorist, however, puts a different case.

Michael Moore

Michael Moore, who once worked at the British Open University, offers a different approach from Peters. His contribution has been in the area of the theory and practice of independent study. Moore associates independent learning with what he calls learning in the individual mode. The early form of individual learning he calls the scholarly tradition. This was broadly the tutorial system associated with the Universities of Oxford and Cambridge.

The contemporary tradition in independent study he calls the 'telemathic'. This means learning at a distance 'designed for adults who live too far from institutions to attend, or are unable to find classes at convenient times, or who prefer 'home study' (Moore, 1980: 18–19). From these beginnings, Moore develops a concept of 'transactional distance' which he says describes the relationship between teacher and learner in independent study learning. Transactional distance is a function of two variables. Dialogue describes the two-way communication between teacher and learner, while structure describes how the teaching programme is designed to meet the individual's learning needs. From this, Moore develops a typology of different kinds of distance-learning programmes, around the concept of transactional distance, in the same way that Paul was able to develop his criterion of openness as a measure of the institutions themselves.

Above all, Moore has stressed that independent learners are autonomous learners, which has major implications for educators.

> Thus adult learners must be treated by educators as autonomous learners who exercise their autonomy at all stages of the program. After helping a learner identify his objectives, the educator aids him to discover the appropriate resources, define relevant goals, and specify evaluative criteria... At each stage, the educator helps the learner to be as active in the educational transaction as he is able. (Moore, 1980: 26)

Moore later developed this into a typology of interaction between learners, teachers and the content of the educational transaction. He identified three types of interaction.

- *Learner–content interaction.* This is the relation between the learner and what he or she is learning, that is, the nature and degree of understanding.
- *Learner–instructor interaction.* This is the relation between the learner and his or her teacher, especially with regard to all the ways in which the teacher tries to enable the learner to learn.
- *Learner–learner interaction.* This is the relation between one learner and another, with or without the presence of the teacher, for example the situation of the peer-group as a stimulus to learning.

Moore suggests that distance-learning programmes need to ensure all of these forms of interaction are maximized in their structure. But he says not all programmes do so.

> The main weakness of many distance-education programmes is their commitment to only one type of medium... when there is only one medium it is probable that only one kind of interaction is permitted or done well... It is vitally important that distance educators in all media do more to plan for all three kinds of interaction, and use the expertise of educators and communication specialists in both traditional media – printed, broadcast, or recorded – and newer teleconference media. (Moore, 1993: 23–24)

We should note that the division of labour (educators, communication specialists) which Otto Peters identified in distance learning is also a feature in Moore's theory. With the advent of specialized computer-generated materials, such specialization is likely to continue to be important.

Börje Holmberg

We have already observed that Holmberg sees distance education as a distinctive mode of education, not merely a sub-category of open learning. In his writings he has developed the themes stressed by Moore, namely, the independent and autonomous character of distance learning. Independence and autonomy are characteristic of all effective learning, according to Holmberg. He has, however, gone further in his analysis of what Moore called the 'educational transaction'. This has considerable practical implications for the design and delivery of distance-learning materials, as we shall see.

Holmberg's basic general assumption is that 'real learning is primarily an individual activity and is attained only through an internalizing process' (Holmberg, 1995: 47). In his analysis of the educational transaction of distance education he has introduced and operationalized the concept of guided didactic conversation.

Put simply, guided didactic conversation is Holmberg's way of describing how the distance educator should communicate with his or her students in order to ensure real learning. He uses an analogy of a conversation to describe the 'distance transaction', and derives seven postulates.

1. That feelings of personal relation between the teaching and learning parties promote study pleasure and motivation.
2. That such feelings can be fostered by well-developed self-instructional material and two-way communication at a distance.
3. That intellectual pleasure and study motivation are favourable to the attainment of study goals and the use of proper study processes and methods.
4. That the atmosphere, language and conventions of friendly conversation favour feelings of personal relation according to postulate 1.
5. That messages given and received in conversational forms are comparatively easily understood and remembered.
6. That the conversation concept can be successfully translated, for use by the media available, to distance education.
7. That planning and guiding the work, whether provided by the teaching organization or the student, are necessary for organizing study, which is characterized by explicit or implicit goal conceptions. (Holmberg, 1995: 47)

As we shall see, Holmberg's seven postulates can be operationalized in the development of distance-learning materials. The remainder of this chapter is concerned with the practical consequences of distance education theory.

From theory to practice

The three theorists whose writings have now been introduced have provided us with three organizing principles for approaching the practice of distance education:

- Peters' account of the division of labour involved in delivering distance education, reflecting an 'industrial' model
- Moore's concepts of independent learning and the autonomy of learners
- Holmberg's concept of guided didactic conversation.

Between them, these constitute the major principles which underpin good practice in all distance education: the organization and administration of the system, the educational relationships between teachers and learners, and the kinds of learning materials and modes of delivery most appropriate to meeting distance students' learning needs.

We shall resume where the theory left off, with Holmberg's own operationalization of his seven postulates of guided didactic conversation.

Distance-learning materials

If we accept his postulates, then certain broad guidelines follow for what Holmberg calls the teaching strategy appropriate to distance-learning materials, and what Moore described as the types of interaction involved in distance education (see above):

- easily accessible presentations of study matter; clear, somewhat colloquial language, in easily readable writing; moderate density of information;
- explicit advice and suggestions to the student as to what to do and what to avoid, what to pay particular attention to and consider, with reasons provided;
- invitations to an exchange of views, to questions, to opinions and comments;
- attempts to involve the student emotionally so that he or she takes a personal interest in the subject and its problems;
- personal style including the use of personal and possessive pronouns: I, my, you, your, etc;
- demarcation of themes through explicit statements, typographical means, or in recorded, spoken communication, through a change of speakers (eg male followed by female) or through pauses. (Holmberg, 1995: 48–49)

These practical guidelines for style in distance-learning materials are increasingly incorporated into study programmes. They are particularly relevant to printed or audio materials. But there is an ever-widening range of both materials and media in distance education. The 'transaction' or 'conversation' between teachers and learners has been further facilitated by the possibilities opened up by the new technologies.

The traditional materials had their origins in correspondence courses, which Peters associated historically with the development of postal services in industrial society. These inevitably represented rather narrow possibilities for communication. As Moore argued, many distance-education programmes are still based upon only one type of medium, although 'the combination of one-way satellite video and two-way audio is increasingly dominant'. (Moore, 1993: 23)

For some time, the standard classification of learning materials has been into printed, audio, video and computer disk. The British Open University pioneered many such materials in the 1970s, and has since continued to develop the possibilities of each of these forms.

- Printed materials continue to be very common, usually in association with other media. Study guides are often combined with texts or edited readings. Their presentation can incorporate many of Holmberg's 'conversational' features, such as illustrations, diagrams, charts, cartoons and so on. They are also structured to include student activities, stimulation to reflection and self-evaluation and guided progression.

- Audio-cassette materials usually supplement the printed ones. They have proved a very flexible source of learning if well produced. The British Open University, of course, has the advantage of radio and television broadcasts to widen the range of media even further.
- Videotapes are now much more accessible to learners. In the British Open University, distance learners are provided with access to science and technology subjects through a combination of videos and experimental kits.
- Computers have also become common in education and training. They open up immense possibilities for interactive learning in fields where demonstration, simulation or learning games are particularly appropriate, such as management and business studies.

Depending upon students' learning needs and the content of the learning, various combinations of these possibilities make possible the kinds of independent learning, autonomy and 'didactic conversation' which our theorists prescribed.

In chapter 2 we described one of the social changes underlying the trend to lifelong learning. This is an increasing focus on style rather than content, on the medium rather than the message. It is apparent that the focus in distance education is shifting from the materials to the media of communication. In a certain sense, the medium is becoming the message. If this is so, it would reinforce Peters' analysis of distance education as the product of its age – in this case, the age of information technology. Many aspects of the distance education 'transaction' are, in practice, being enhanced by technology. Already electronic mail, audio-conferencing, tele-conferencing and video-conferencing are overtaking the postal and telephone communications systems. These make for instant interaction between teachers and learners, whilst the Internet may prove one of the most significant of all sources of lifelong learning.

Conclusion

In this chapter we have reviewed some important theoretical contributions to open and distance learning. Otto Peters, Michael Moore and Börje Holmberg have all offered different insights into what makes distance education a distinctive form of learning, although the implications of their theories have not been fully developed in relation to more recent advances in information technology.

We have also reviewed some of the implications for practice arising from these theoretical contributions, and described some of the principles of good practice with regard to the development of distance-learning programmes.

Chapter 12

Work-based and problem-based learning

Learning at work

There has been a recurring theme in debates about education over the years. How should schools prepare children for the 'world of work'? Do they do so effectively? But the fact that schools (and colleges, professional institutes and universities) are designed to educate or train for work – among other things – has tended to obscure another truth. People do not just learn in order to work. They learn at work. For most jobs, workers require some skills from the outset. For some jobs, a lot of prior knowledge is essential. But learning does not stop when you walk through the office or factory door for the first time.

In fact, as almost everyone knows, starting a new job calls for rapid learning. New members of staff have to find out, in double quick time, about the geography of the workplace, the routines and demands of the job, and relationships with managers and colleagues. They are given – or have to give themselves – a 'crash course' in all of these and more. And learning does not stop when this particular crash course is over. Every workplace changes, and every worker has to learn about and from these changes.

Rather strangely, this fact has only been widely recognized quite recently. Until the last few years, when researchers looked at 'learning', they were usually interested in what happened to children and young people. They concentrated on schools, colleges and universities. When they turned to learning in workplace contexts, they concentrated on what happens in 'formal' training situations: company training departments, day-release programmes and so forth. They showed little concern with what men and women learn from day to day in their work.

The growing realization of how important learning is at work has begun to change this. Researchers have now begun to look at how people learn in the workplace, and not just in formal educational or training contexts. In this chapter, we explore why understandings of learning at work have changed so radically. We begin with a brief history of learning at work. Then we examine what we now know about learning at work, both formal and informal. Finally, we look at how new understandings of learning at work have influenced approaches to preparing them for work. The main example of this is problem-based learning. In professional education, management education, role education of various kinds, and trade-union and labour education, learning is now commonly based around the consideration and analysis of 'real' problems and case studies.

A brief history of learning at work

No archaeologist would be surprised to discover that people learn at work. No-one who has tried to chip a stone axe, and compared the product with axe-heads fashioned by Neolithic craftsmen, underestimates the sophistication of Stone-Age work skills. These skills, developed and improved over thousands of human generations, have now been largely lost. Human societies have always been characterized by two features. We develop and use technologies: we innovate. But just as important – indeed, arguably much more so – we communicate knowledge and expertise about these technologies to other people. We innovate; but we also carry out the innovations of others (often with their guidance). Both of these involve learning.

How human societies organize work-related learning depends on how they organize work. In ancient and medieval western societies, for example, agricultural production was typically organized around household and kinship networks. There was little specialization, and work-related learning took place within the household and family setting. A few activities were carried out separately, because they required particular forms of technology, skill or expertise: farriers, blacksmiths, millers and so on. Nobles, with their greater wealth, enabled a few, still-more specialized, trades to prosper: jewellers, falconers, court jesters and armourers. These specialized craft skills were developed chiefly through apprenticeship. Over a long period, often seven or more years, beginning in childhood but continuing until early adulthood, the apprentice learnt the trade through attachment to a master craftsman.

Partly for mutual protection, partly for what we should today call quality assurance reasons, these craftsmen banded together in guilds. Guilds set standards, particularly by insisting on apprenticeship. They also provided a focus for sharing and valuing specialist professional or technical knowledge. They were, therefore, a vital support for learning and technical innovation in the craft industries of early modern Europe.

Capitalist production changed this. As Adam Smith and Karl Marx both recognized, what distinguished capitalist production was its 'division of labour' within the workplace. Capitalists did not just employ workers. In the factories of the nineteenth and twentieth centuries, they controlled how workers produced goods. They organized the production process, and in order to do this they needed to know how to make things. This was a type of knowledge previously confined to craftsmen.

Having this knowledge, of course, was not enough. They used it to design production processes. This meant that much of the knowledge had to be distributed again to workers. But it was distributed in a particular way. Where craft skills had encompassed the entire production process, factory workers were now to know only what they needed to know to carry out a specific task. Of course, there were a few specialists who knew much more (managers, engineers and so forth). These people became the new élite, but they were very much the agents of the owners.

This completely changed what learning was required. Workers should now know as little as necessary, rather than as much as possible. The source of knowledge was to be the employer and his organization, rather than other workers. Of course, workers continued to learn a lot informally, but only from other workers with very closely defined work roles. Even informal learning was largely defined by the segmented character of the factory.

There were variations, of course. In some manufacturing processes it was quite easy to control the organization of work and knowledge. In others it was much harder. The typical factory would have some highly skilled workers (who might have served long apprenticeships), and others who were only 'semi-skilled' or even 'unskilled'. Skilled workers – compositors in printing and maintenance trades in many industries, for instance – were employed, but only to carry out critical tasks which it was impossible, or excessively costly, for employers to take over. Because the employer relied very heavily on their abilities, skilled workers were typically paid significantly more. In return, they were trusted to organize their own pace and pattern of work.

For much of the nineteenth and twentieth centuries, employers' attitudes to learning at work were founded on these key realities. Most workers should know only what they needed to know to complete the tasks they were set. For them, training was very limited. A smaller number of more highly skilled workers required more training. They were supported through apprenticeship schemes and the like. Employers' attitudes could be influenced by other factors. For instance, training might encourage workers to be loyal when competition for labour was fierce, or when trade unions threatened. But the fundamentals of training were clear: little for the many; rather more for the few.

Training and the changing workplace

For most managers of the nineteenth and twentieth centuries, the road to effective organization lay through bureaucracy and hierarchy. The essence of the methods popularized by such men as F W Taylor and Henry Ford was that the people at the top made decisions on the basis of rational analysis and planning. The people lower down carried out the tasks they were allotted. Such an image of what makes an organization work well had very clear implications for training. According to one popular management text of the 1950s and 1960s, '85 per cent of all industrial jobs in the USA could be learnt in a fortnight' (Hooper, 1960: 34).

This model has clear implications for how much training should be given. It also influenced what should be taught and how. Managers, especially top managers, required sophisticated technical skills: budgeting, strategy and planning, engineering and so forth. Training for others was defined by their roles – and could often be 'read off' from their job descriptions. When training developed in the twentieth-century company, therefore – chiefly after the Second World War – it emerged in a highly stratified way. There was a system for senior managers, or those expected to become senior managers. There was another for middle managers, another for skilled workers and yet another for the unskilled.

One key difference between these types of training was where they took place. For managers, especially those on the career ladder to senior positions, training was largely conducted outside the company. It was strongly influenced by government and professional associations. For instance, the British Institute of Management collaborated with the Ministry of Education to establish curricula for further education colleges, while the Administrative Staff College at Henley provided more advanced courses. From the 1960s, universities began to seek a role, following the model of university business schools in the USA. In contrast, training for workers was provided largely within companies, and generally as just one of the 'personnel' functions. Employers alone determined what the training needs of their junior staff were.

In the 1960s, bureaucratic and 'scientific' approaches to management began to be criticized. Writers such as Tom Burns and Joan Woodward challenged the idea that there was one best form of organization. Which form of organization was most effective depended, they said, on such factors as the nature of the production process, and the technological and market situation of the enterprise. In many enterprises, it was quite unrealistic to think that knowledge could effectively be centralized. Success depended upon the middle and lower ranges of management, and even workers themselves, having substantial amounts of discretion and autonomy. Such companies had to trust their workers to make sensible judgements in the best interests of the organization.

Four considerations became apparent from this. First, the clear dividing line between managers (who make decisions) and workers (who do what they are told) began to break down. Second, it became very difficult to prescribe in advance all the types of knowledge which a worker – and still less a manager – might require. Third, it placed emphasis on the changing commercial and technological environment, rather than suggesting that the company should attempt to control this environment. Fourth, training could not be merely technical. Its function was to generate the trainee's commitment to the ideals and aims of the organization. In the technical language of learning theory, it had to be affective as well as cognitive.

Since the 1960s, it has become ever more apparent that companies cannot control their environments. The pace of technological and market change has quickened, and with the birth of the knowledge society an increasing number of workers are using knowledge rather than skills (Stehr, 1994; Reich, 1991). Successful firms adapt to and learn from their environments. To do so they must rely on their workers.

Developing 'human resources'

Of course, if successful firms rely heavily on their workers, their workers become more important. This realization lay behind the emergence of 'human resources' as a concept. Workers were not just 'personnel' – necessary evils in the production process – but 'resources' on which the organization actively depended. There was a good measure of tokenism in this, to be sure. Many human resources departments were merely 'personnel' with a vogueish new title. Many books on 'human resources development' merely reproduced the common currency of training. Yet overall, the shift in emphasis was vital.

In this new approach, several features stand out. First, human resources may need to be developed, but they are only valuable if they remain committed to the organization. A key dimension of human resources development (HRD), therefore, is to persuade staff that their interests and those of the company are one and the same. Second, training had brought formal, planned learning into the workplace. Human resources development retains the idea of planning, but extends it into the informal, into learning rather than training. Third, the uncertainty which demanded new, decentralized, approaches to organization and management also meant that knowledge had to be differently managed within the organization. Training could no longer consist of the transmission of relevant parts of a body of centrally held information. If staff are expected to make their own judgements in responding to unpredictable situations, training (or learning) programmes can hardly consist of telling them in detail what to do.

The new concern with the planning of learning, rather than teaching, meant that HRD specialists began to look at how learning should be organized. They approached this with the techniques of rational programme planning derived from education and training. On the face of it, these held promise. The concept of training need easily became a learning need. Training aims and objectives translated quite straightforwardly into learning aims and objectives. Evaluating whether objectives had been achieved and 'needs reduced' was as applicable to learning as to training. But a new approach was needed in the organization and delivery of training activities. A trainer can organize broadly common training activities for large groups of people. Ensuring that different people have common learning experiences is far more difficult – indeed, arguably impossible.

It would be an exaggeration to say this difficulty has been overcome. But the direction in which HRD has sought a solution is now apparent. It consists of asking workers to use their judgement more, but to do so responsibly. The key question, of course, is how this 'responsibility' is to be ensured. The answer has been twofold. On the one hand, it is now asserted strongly – so strongly that almost no-one now doubts it – that learning benefits the worker as much as, or more than, the employer. Workers and employers therefore have a common interest in learning. On the other, the idea of 'contract' has been brought in to minimize the room for error between what it is intended should be learnt and what actually is learnt. (We have discussed contracts in more detail in chapter 10.)

One result of this trend has been a developing interest in what people learn in workplace environments, and how. It is to these concerns we now turn. A number of emphases emerge for consideration. We begin by looking at the development of problem-based approaches to learning. This can be seen as asking how classrooms can be made to reflect the real problems of workplaces. Next we look at action learning, which was one of the first attempts to integrate learning into the work situation. Then we turn to the more recent developments in our knowledge of informal and incidental learning in workplaces. A further and important development from this line of thinking, the idea of the 'learning organization', is dealt with on its own in chapter 13.

Problem-based learning

Work-related learning has two rather distinct aspects. For some writers, the key issue is how we can make learning in classrooms properly reflect the real world of work. The most important trend in this area is problem-based learning. Boud and Feletti define this as 'constructing and teaching courses using problems as the stimulus and focus for student activity'. Problem-based learning does not simply bring problem solving into a traditional curriculum based on disciplines. It builds a curriculum around key problems in professional practice.

> Problem-based courses start with problems rather than with the exposition of disciplinary knowledge. They move students towards the acquisition of knowledge and skills through a staged sequence of problems presented in context, together with associated learning materials and support from teachers. (Boud and Feletti, 1991: 14)

Boud and Feletti (1991: 14) locate the origins of problem-based learning in the health sciences, citing US and Canadian medical schools in the 1950s and 1960s. But similar trends can be found in other (perhaps less prestigious) sectors. From the early 1950s, for example, British trade-union educators developed an approach which proceeded 'through a consideration of specific and concrete problems in which the major points to be dealt with are taken very deliberately and amply illustrated in a practical way' (WEA, 1953: 58; see also Holford, 1994).

The key to problem-based learning is using material through which students engage with problems in situations as near as possible to 'real life'. This means that, in terms of traditional educational organization, it crosses disciplinary boundaries. Students typically (though not always) work collaboratively in small groups or teams to clarify and define the nature of the problem, and how they can deal with it. They normally have access to resource material. They are often supported by a tutor; he or she may be a facilitator rather than an expert in the field. If specific areas of learning need are identified, these are addressed through providing resource material of the relevant kind.

Advocates of strong versions of problem-based learning argue that it should not be thought of as a method, but as an entire approach to learning. Engel (1991: 29) outlines four key elements of a problem-based curriculum.

- Learning is seen as cumulative. Subjects and topics are not studied in depth at one time. Instead, they are repeatedly introduced with increasing sophistication whenever they contribute to a process of decision making on a problem.

- Learning is integrated. Subjects are not presented separately, but are available for investigation at the time they are seen to relate to a problem.
- There is progression in learning. The various elements of the curriculum (such as the use and make-up of groups, the relationship of theory to practice) change as the students mature and progress.
- Learning must be consistent. The aims of problem-based learning should be supported in every aspect of the curriculum and its implementation. For example, students should be treated throughout as responsible adults, and summative assessment should therefore be used sparingly, and should test application of knowledge, not just recall.

Such an approach makes demands on the organization of educational institutions and on curriculum planning. Within universities, colleges and schools, for instance, authority must shift away from disciplines toward inter-disciplinary or multi-disciplinary groupings of staff. But curricula still need to be designed, and students' educational progression monitored. Structures (committees, working groups and the like) are necessary for this. However, Engel argues that these should not be formed on the basis of subject representation. A key element in the construction of problem-based progress routes is formulating generalizable competencies. These are based clearly on the kind of abilities and skills which a professional practitioner will need on completion of the qualification.

The core of problem-based learning is its emphasis on contextuality. Problems can be understood, and approaches to solving them devised, only in context. However, not all contexts are problematic, as Argyris and Schön's double-loop learning (1974) indicates. From a learning theory perspective, this places problem-based learning firmly in the experiential learning, constructivist tradition. Professional tasks involve the application of knowledge in context. The knowledge has no meaning (or at any rate a different meaning) unless it is applied and contextualized in this way. The professionals or students who devise solutions to the problems posed are, in an important sense, constructing new knowledge as they do so.

Action learning

In one sense, problem-based learning is about how classrooms, and what goes on inside them, can be made to reflect what workplaces are really like. We look next at some researchers who have almost turned this question around. They have asked how workplaces themselves can be made better learning environments. Posed rather more starkly, how can we make workplaces into (good) classrooms?

The shift in the workplace from 'training' to 'learning' has posed the problem of how to generate an organized and comprehensive approach to what is essentially an individual process. But it also raised a very specific and practical difficulty. Even as late as the mid-1980s, rather little was known about learning in workplace contexts. Training in industry had remained a generally low-status activity, and had generated little serious research. Management training had been rather more studied (we return to this below). But even there the concerns had been less with how managers learnt, and more with what managers should know, and how they should be taught – the nature of the curriculum.

In fact, as early as the 1950s there had been a pioneering and very important attempt to develop a new approach to learning at work. This was action learning, a mode of work-based learning developed by Reg Revans, then working with Britain's National Coal Board, though now a distinguished management philosopher. This approach has proved very influential, particularly in management education and development. It has also been adopted in educational courses, especially for mature adult learners (eg Weil and McGill, 1989).

Action learning involves, not surprisingly, a commitment to action. Indeed Revans suggests that verbal explanations cannot convey the nature of action learning for those who have not tried it in practice. At the same time he emphasizes its simplicity – in essence it is 'learning by doing'. His central thesis is that 'responsible action is our greatest disciplinarian as well as our most sympathetic helper' (1983: 20).

Lessem (1993) suggests that Revans' approach has its roots in the empiricism of Francis Bacon, the entrepreneurial of Adam Smith, and the self-improvement philosophy of Samuel Smiles. His writing makes much use of biblical quotes and references.

Action learning is, significantly, a social process. Revans states for example (1983: 11):

> It is recognized ignorance not programmed knowledge that is the key to action learning: men start to learn with and from each other only when they discover that no-one knows the answer but all are obliged to find it.

From this principle comes the idea of the action-learning set, a group in which members are 'comrades in adversity' and support each other in their action learning.

Revans also emphasizes the role of systematic research in action learning and sees it as building on, rather than aiming to replace, the academic tradition. However, it is 'real-time' learning process, a means by which managers engage in problem solving in the workplace and test their proposals through implementation. For Revans, therefore, action is almost the sea in which learners swim. It is only through action that we can bridge our subjective worlds with social reality.

While Revans is the key name in this field, his contribution appears to be acknowledged more in the practical than the academic arena. His hurt is evident. Commenting on developments that bear similarity to action learning but which have been given different labels, he said 'it is only when I refer to the date of such accounts (usually in the past couple of years) that I can be assured that my writings of the 1950s are not unconscious plagiarism' (1983: 20).

Informal and incidental learning

During the late 1980s and early 1990s, some researchers saw the need to establish a new research focus on learning in workplace contexts. Victoria Marsick (1987) gathered contributions from a number of researchers and practitioners on the topic of learning in the workplace. She argued that a 'new paradigm' for workplace learning could be developed, chiefly by combining the practical insights of various emerging trends in workplaces with contributions from adult education theory (particularly the work of Jack Mezirow). Traditional applications of learning theory in work-related settings had, she argued, been based on a behaviouristic paradigm. This involved: a 'behavioural performance focus on cause–effect actions' that were quantifiable, criterion-referenced and measurable; a separation of personal development from work-related development; a 'deficit' model in the design of learning activities; a 'linear problem-solving emphasis'; a preference for standardized group activities; and a focus on 'pure' learning problems supplemented by manipulation of the learning environment to support outcomes (Marsick, 1987: 24).

Marsick's 'new paradigm' contained a number of elements.

- Work-related learning should go beyond what can be derived from behaviouristic models of learning. Men and women at work also learn about 'consensual norms through dialogue' and learn about themselves 'by reflecting on their identity *vis-à-vis* work and the organization'. Individuals are most productive when contributing to shared organizational goals which are 'personally meaningful'.
- People learn best about work when their own 'identity and growth' are seen as integral to the learning.
- The organizations most conducive to learning are flexible, those where all employees are encouraged to learn many aspects of the work and participate jointly in decentralized decision making.
- The 'unit for learning' was not just the individual, but groups within the organization. Teamwork is valued not simply to reach pre-defined goals, but to create new goals in pursuit of enhanced productivity.

- Learning design should emphasize reflectivity and creativity: individuals should be encouraged to develop 'a habit of reflectivity in both formal and informal learning modes'.
- Participation in setting the problems for learning is as important in this paradigm as is finding the best solution'. (Marsick, 1987: 25)

There is a stronger emphasis on helping individuals and groups to learn through understanding their daily informal interactions and using them for personal and professional development.

> The organization is considered a learning environment for the growth of individuals and groups *vis-à-vis* work, not solely as a factor to be manipulated to produce desired behaviour. As a learning environment, it must provide opportunities for experimentation, risk-taking, dialogue, initiative, creativity and participation in decision making. (Marsick, 1987: 25)

What Marsick argued, then, was not that organizations and workplaces enhance learning, but that some workplaces and organizations do so. The types of organizational environment conducive to learning turn out – in her view – to be remarkably similar to those which Burns and Stalker first began to notice in the 1960s: those which rely heavily on the judgement and autonomy of their staff. Since the 1960s many management writers have claimed that organizations like these are best adapted for a global, knowledge-centred, rapidly changing society. Hales (1993: 164) refers to these as 'adhocratic' organizations. He says they pursue 'innovation, problem solving and responsiveness to situational demands through the creation of a loose federation of temporary work units, or teams, in which technical expertise and creativity are given free rein'. Many popular management texts now argue the superiority of this type of organization. Often they are quite small firms in knowledge-based industries. Their effectiveness stems from harnessing teams for creative purposes rather than from undertaking routine and repetitive tasks.

One difficulty with this approach is that it can seem to do little more than describe the characteristics of a certain type of organization. Certainly some organizations rely heavily on knowledge, and they need to encourage their staff to use information creatively. Not surprisingly, such organizations work best when they encourage their staff to handle information in creative ways. But when information is processed by people in creative ways, are we not just using other words to describe the fact that they are learning? We may develop a special language to describe the people who work in such workplaces and some of the things they do – facilitators, mentors, collegial learning environments, consulting and so forth. But though this may be interesting, does it help us to create good learning environments? In other words, is a good learning environment something which we can make – as, for example, we can design a school classroom? Or is it just something which exists or does not?

This depends, of course, on what factors 'cause' organizations to take certain forms. There have been many views on this. Some sociologists and management theorists (eg Burns and Stalker, 1961) have argued that technology is a key factor. Others have seen the market position of the firm as vital (Burns and Stalker, 1961). More recent writers have emphasized the role of organizational size, age, goals and other factors (Handy, 1989; Mintzberg, 1979). While there is room for disagreement on this, the broad thrust of these 'contingency theorists' is that organizational structures evolve in relation to structural factors, rather than as a result of free choice by managers. We return to this issue below.

If certain forms of workplace environment encourage learning, as Marsick argues, two issues clearly arise. First, are certain kinds of people more likely to learn in these contexts than others? If so, what is it about these people that makes them more likely to learn? Do they have particular attitudes, or learning styles, for instance? Can people adapt (or be changed) to make them more likely to learn? Second, can we redesign workplaces in order to make them better learning environments?

Marsick and Watkins (1990) addressed the first question in their book *Informal and Incidental Learning in the Workplace*. They argued that while some attention had been devoted to the training process, there had been little rigorous analysis of other forms of workplace learning. They then distinguished informal from incidental learning. Informal learning is mainly experiential and takes place in non-institutional settings, but is often planned. Examples include self-directed learning, networking, coaching, mentoring, and performance planning. Incidental learning is unintentional, the by-product of another activity. Examples would be when people learn from mistakes, assumptions, beliefs or the 'hidden curriculum'.

Informal learning is enhanced, they argued, when individuals are 'proactive', 'creative' and engage in 'critical reflection'. Proactivity is a matter of looking for opportunities: seeing unpredicted situations as opportunities for learning, rather than rejecting the new because it is not meaningful. Creativity might involve seeking new approaches to learning. It might also mean having creative hobbies (music, painting or writing) or the individuals considering themselves 'creative intrapreneurs or entrepreneurs' (Marsick and Watkins, 1990: 219). Critical reflectivity allows them to challenge the assumptions and norms which lie behind their thinking and action.

The difficulty with incidental learning, according to Marsick and Watkins, is that what people learn incidentally is not 'inherently correct'. They give an example of trainers who found that when approached to allow more time for training, managers always said no. The trainers learnt – incidentally – that it was not worth asking for more training time. Yet although this was 'true', it was also not true – because systems and organizational cultures are, they say, always in flux. The best incidental learners, therefore, are those who can bring their 'tacit theories' and beliefs to the surface. When they come to the surface, we can make conscious decisions about whether or not to change them.

According to Watkins and Marsick, then, there are some things which individuals can do to make themselves better informal and incidental learners. These include:

- 'surfacing' tacit theories;
- identifying assumptions and associations we have made about other people or situations, and looking for examples which will support or challenge these assumptions;
- problematizing situations: taking familiar situations and thinking about them as though they were problematic or unfamiliar;
- engaging in deliberately reflective, transformative learning;
- seeking public support of disconfirmation of our private theories;
- trying to take a holistic, long-term view of a problem or task.

This, then, is what individuals can do to make themselves better learners. But can we make organizations into better learning environments? According to Watkins and Marsick, things can be done at both group and organizational levels. Groups need to engage in double-loop learning, reassessing the 'assumptions and goals on which they base their actions' (Marsick and Watkins, 1990: 228). Organizations which promote learning are those where 'active interaction among employees, work teams and managers is institutionalized'. This involves 'helping first-time managers make role transitions, by consciously timing job enlargements or promotions for optimum growth, by helping with critical transitions – especially in dealing with complexity and increasing scope – and by making corrections' (Marsick and Watkins, 1990: 230–31).

Having said this, however, a number of criticisms of Marsick and Watkins' position need to be considered. First, while describing the types of organization in which learning is maximized, they do not show that such organizations can be constructed. This is the argument from contingency theory, which we discussed earlier. Even if we know that certain types of organization are best for encouraging learning, this does not mean that these types of organization are 'the best'. Marsick and Watkins' ideal organization is what Hales calls 'adhocracy'. Yet, as he points out, 'in whatever form, adhocracy is rare and has not supplanted bureaucracy in the way that some predicted' (Hales, 1993: 171). In their more recent work, Marsick and Watkins have pursued the holy grail of changing organizational forms by advocating the 'learning organization'. We discuss this concept further in chapter 13.

Second, although they write of informal and incidental learning in the workplace, Marsick and Watkins concentrate on two types of learners: managers and professionals. Their detailed case studies relate to managers, community educators, human resource developers and higher education administrators – not to textile or assembly plant workers, hotel or hospital cleaners, security guards or waiters. One result, arguably, is that they overvalue the types of learning required by managers and professionals, and underplay the learning required to cope in more routine and oppressive work situations.

Finally, a number of authors have argued that the entire movement toward establishing learning organizations is ideological. From this view, all the easy talk about learning organizations is little more than the latest in a long history of measures designed to maintain the authority of managers, and weaken workers. This is a theme we shall return to toward the end of the next chapter.

Chapter 13

The learning organization

by Paul Tosey

If we are becoming a learning society, many would argue that organizations play an important role. The theme of the 'learning organization' has attracted significant international interest in recent years.

Contemporary interest in the learning organization dates from the mid-1980s. In an article published in Britain in 1989, Pedler *et al.* noted that the term learning organization had begun to enter mainstream thinking. A closely related but not identical term, 'organizational learning', can be traced back to the work of Chris Argyris and Donald Schön (Argyris, 1992; Argyris and Schön, 1978). For example, these authors said, in the late 1970s:

> There has probably never been a time in our history where members, managers and students of organizations were so united on the importance of organizational learning. (Argyris and Schön, 1978; cited by Butler in Burgoyne *et al.*, 1994)

In this chapter we discuss both these ideas. We look at where they came from and how they are defined. We discuss possible reasons for the contemporary prominence of the learning organization. The key contributions of leading authors in the field are discussed, together with examples of practical application. Finally, we raise some critical questions about this field and its relevance to the main themes of the book.

The historical evolution of the learning organization

The importance of learning for organizations has changed over time. A particular factor has been changing ideas about the nature of organizations and management. For example, in classic bureaucratic organizations learning is strongly linked to professionalization. Swieringa and Wierdsma (1992: 140) argue that the concept of the learning organization may be a response to the outdatedness of the bureaucratic form of organization, where hierarchical stratification separates thinking, deciding, doing and reflecting.

In the 'scientific' view of organizations, usually associated with Taylorism from the early twentieth century (see Morgan 1997), the emphasis was likely to be on the acquisition of technical skills for task efficiency. A different and often conflicting emphasis emerged through the human relations movement and, subsequently, with the work of authors such as Abraham Maslow and Douglas McGregor. This helped to spark interest in the learning and personal development of individuals in organizations. This emphasis grew in the 1960s and 1970s through the emerging field of organizational development, and concurrent interest in the quality of working life.

In very broad terms, according to metaphors identified by Gareth Morgan (1997), there has been a shift from seeing organizations as machines towards seeing organizations as organic systems or even brains. Learning is seen less as an input intended to make the machine more efficient. After all, if an organization is like a brain or an organism, learning is very much one of its inherent components.

Pedler *et al.* place the theme of the learning organization in an historical context. They trace the progression of training and development work through a number of eras. They argue that 'systematic training, self-development and creating learning companies are approaches that have responded to contemporary problems, and either created, or revealed, the next problem' (Burgoyne *et al.*, 1994: 2).

In the 1960s and 1970s learning became especially prominent in the field of management development, particularly through the action learning work of Reg Revans (see chapter 12). Revans is also know for his formulation of a central idea in this movement. 'For an organization to survive,' he wrote, 'its rate of learning must be equal to or greater than the rate of change in its external environment' (quoted in Garratt, 1987: 54).

Undoubtedly Revans and others are important influences on the idea of the learning organization. But they were still concerned with the effectiveness of individual learning, albeit of individuals located within organizations. Their contribution has therefore been covered in chapter 12.

So, learning has always had a role in organizations. What has changed is the nature of that role, and the extent to which learning is viewed as a core component of organizations. As we have seen, it was in the 1980s that the theme of the learning organization became highly popular. But why did the idea of learning become so prevalent in the organizational and business world at that time? The following factors seem to be significant.

Growing acceptance of the idea that change is a constant

The theme of a rapidly increasing rate of change is by no means new. Alvin Toffler's *Future Shock* (1970) raised this issue in the early 1970s. But, as a broad generalization, many businesses have come to accept that change is not a temporary interlude between periods of stability.

Increasingly, authors such as Charles Handy (eg 1989) have told us that we cannot rely on the same ideas that served us in the past. Handy has suggested, for example, that we need to rethink our assumptions about what an organization is. Instead of the typical organization consisting of people gathered together in the same physical location, he envisages a 'shamrock' organization. Here the continuing core of people may be very small. Many functions and services will be distributed or sub-contracted. Many people may never meet face to face or be in the same geographical location. Instead communications will be at a distance through information technology.

Thus rapid change, whether 'objectively' real or just perceived, has created a number of challenges or problems to which learning may be seen as the solution. Businesses may have a shorter time in which to adapt to changes in the market and to changes in technology. They have to develop new products and practices quickly if they are not to go out of business. It is now accepted that a company or industry which drags its feet will swiftly become uncompetitive. The American motor-manufacturing industry, for example, suffered in the 1970s and 1980s from the combined effect of failing to take seriously the growing concern for ecology, which led to consumer preferences for smaller cars, and the new manufacturing expertise of Japanese companies.

This has led some writers to propose general (rather than specific and testable) links between learning and organizational success. For example, Stata says he:

> would argue that the rate at which individuals and organizations learn may become the only sustainable competitive advantage, especially in knowledge-intensive industries. (Stata, 1994: 356)

The 'post-industrial era' and the need for a flexible workforce

As the nature of organization and work changes, so does the nature of employment. There has been increasing emphasis on the need for a flexible workforce. When employees need to adapt quickly and keep up to date with new skills, learning becomes an essential core competence. The very relationship between employers and employees (sometimes referred to as the 'psychological contract') is thought to be changing. People used to enter occupations expecting to stay in the same line of work for life. Often they stayed with the same company or organization. Now people seem to be expected to move from occupation to occupation, re-training according to the work opportunities available.

Of course, this means different things to different people. Some argue that this type of learning reflects an attitudinal change and enables employers to loosen their responsibilities to employees. Burgoyne *et al.* refer to 'divisions of labour between people shifting and breaking down in the post-industrial era, the era of the flexible firm' (1994: 3).

Advances in understanding of how organizations change

A third possible factor is that we now know more about how organizations change and what makes them effective. When organizations were perceived as machines, the issues were to do with design and technology. While many people do still take an 'engineering' approach to organizational functioning, the twentieth century has also seen growing sophistication of thinking about organizations as human systems. For example David Casey, a consultant with the Ashridge Management College in Britain, said:

> We notice that significant organization change does not seem to be achieved when experts from outside an organization deliver analytical diagnoses and make closed recommendations. Significant change seems to occur only when significant learning takes place within the client organization. (Casey, 1993: 71)

There may be a further factor. Managerial development in organizations is seen to be more and more important. This may have led people to conclude that learning should spread from a managerial élite to all employees, and thus raise the overall capacity for learning.

Defining the learning organization

The theme of learning has become very prominent in the world of organizations, and we have explored possible reasons for this. It is more difficult to pin down precisely what is meant by the learning organization.

Learning has many different connotations in the organizational field. Burgoyne *et al.* (1994) affirm the 'multi-directional' nature of the term and its development. Accordingly, there are many proposed definitions of learning organizations. For example, Pedler, Boydell and Burgoyne define the learning company as:

> an organization which facilitates the learning of all its members and continually transforms itself. (Pedler *et al.*, 1989: 2)

This suggests that being a learning organization includes, but is more than, encouraging the learning of individual employees. Watkins and Marsick build on this type of definition and incorporate several themes into their depiction of the learning organization:

> The learning organization is one that learns continuously and transforms itself. Learning takes place in individuals, teams, the organization and even the communities with which the organization interacts. Learning is a continuous, strategically used process – integrated with, and running parallel to, work. Learning results in changes in knowledge, beliefs and behaviours. Learning also enhances organizational capacity for innovation and growth. The learning organization has embedded systems to capture and share learning. (Watkins and Marsick, 1993: 8–9)

This leads us to consider the relationship between the learning organization and organizational learning. Definitions of the former focus on what this type of organization appears to be, and how it is characterized. The latter is concerned more with the 'how' of learning – the processes through which learning takes place.

Swieringa and Wierdsma say:

> By the term 'organizational learning' we mean the changing of organizational behaviour. The changing of organizational behaviour is a collective learning process – an organization has not automatically learnt when individuals within it have learnt something. Individual learning is a necessary but not sufficient condition for organizational learning. (Swieringa and Wierdsma, 1992: 33)

This definition differentiates organizational learning, as a collective process, from individual learning. Is thinking about the learning organization concerned with collective learning processes? Not necessarily. Learning organization seems to denote a wider category that includes ideas, analysis and prescription about the nature of organizations and how they can be effective. Much more is to be found there than concern with processes of learning alone. Jones and Hendry (1992: iv) say that 'learning organization theorists concentrate on the "soft" rather than the "hard" measures in looking at organizational development'. Roth and Niemi (1996) identify three prominent themes in the literature of the learning organization. These are:

- adaptation, change and environmental alignment of organizations
- the multiple levels of learning within organizations
- interpretation, meaning and the world view of organizations.

Landmark contributors

Among the many writers in this field, we identify three as having made particularly important contributions. Other leading authors are referenced elsewhere in this chapter.

Chris Argyris

Although his work predates the re-emergence of the learning organization concept, Chris Argyris remains a key author in the field. His work, both individually (eg Argyris, 1992) and jointly with Donald Schön (Argyris and Schön, 1978) on single-loop and double-loop learning – itself based on the work of Ashby (1952) and Bateson (1973) – underpins or has influenced significantly the thinking of many subsequent writers (eg Garratt, 1987; Hawkins, 1991; Senge, 1990).

Argyris and Schön (1978) did not attempt to define a learning organization. Instead, they posed the question, 'what is an organization that it may learn?' This remains a good question. Morgan (1997) among others points out that when we talk of organizations acting, we anthropomorphize. In other words, we think and talk of organizations as if they were individual human beings. It is one of many metaphors we use to grasp the complexity of organizations but, like any metaphor or analogy, it has its limitations. Thus Argyris and Schön caution that 'organizations do not literally remember, think or learn', and suggest that 'organizational learning might be understood as the testing and restructuring of organizational theories of action'. By 'theory of action' they mean a set of principles aimed at making events come about (1978: 10). Argyris and Schön distinguish between two types of theory of action, which they call espoused theory and theory-in-use. They say:

> When someone is asked how he would behave under certain circumstances, the answer he usually gives is his espoused theory of action for that situation. This is the theory of action to which he gives allegiance and which, upon request, he communicates to others. However, the theory that actually governs his actions is his theory-in-use, which may or may not be compatible with his espoused theory; furthermore, the individual may or may not be aware of the incompatibility of the two theories. (Argyris and Schön, 1978: 11)

Many sources (eg Morgan, 1997) summarize the basic ideas such as single-loop learning. Argyris and Schön define this as what happens when:

> members of the organization respond to changes in the internal and external environments of the organization by detecting errors which they then correct so as to maintain the central features of organizational theory-in-use. (Argyris and Schön, 1978: 18)

In single-loop learning, which is concerned mainly with the achievement of goals, the assumptions and values behind the theory-in-use are not questioned. These are, instead, the focus of double-loop learning. Therefore double-loop learning will result in changes to underlying aims, norms and policies.

Argyris' contribution has been to explore in depth and detail the processes through which organizational learning takes place, and to emphasize the importance for organizations of learning how to learn in both single-loop and double-loop modes.

Mike Pedler, John Burgoyne and Tom Boydell

In Britain, leading thinkers in the field have been Mike Pedler, John Burgoyne and Tom Boydell. They have convened a series of 'learning company' conferences, the first of which took place in 1991.

The approach of Pedler *et al.* is eclectic, as they acknowledge in the first section of their book *The Learning Company* (Pedler *et al.*, 1991). For example, they draw strongly on total quality management. For these authors, it seems that the learning organization is a theme in the evolving history of organizational ideas, not an identifiable theory or a specifiable practice.

The learning company is described in two ways. The first is a schematic depiction of flows of information through policy, operations, ideas and action, which Pedler *et al.* call the 'energy flow model' (1991: 32). The second has the following eleven characteristics:

- a learning strategy;
- a high level of participation in policy making by organizational members and stakeholders;
- use of information technology for sharing knowledge and mutual awareness;
- accounting and control processes which give feedback helpful to understanding the effects of action, to learning and decision-making;
- internal 'customer/client' relationships feeding mutual adjustment and adaptation;
- reward systems consistent with an employment philosophy, which includes the incentivization of learning;
- forms of structure which enable learning and can shift, adapt and accommodate change resulting from it;
- boundary workers – people working at the formal boundaries of the organization, collecting and passing on 'environmental' information, involving external stakeholders in improving organizational processes;
- willingness and ability to learn with and from other organizations and companies;
- a culture and climate which encourage responsible experimentation and shared learning from successes and failures;
- mechanisms and employee relationships which encourage and support self-development. (Burgoyne *et al.*, 1994: 4)

Pedler *et al.* have contributed greatly by looking at what is meant in practice by a learning organization, and by bringing together academics, consultants and managers to look at this theme.

Peter Senge

A leading author has undoubtedly been Peter Senge, from the USA. His book *The Fifth Discipline* (1990), subtitled 'The Art and Practice of the Learning Organization', has probably done more than any other book to bring the idea of the learning organization to popular attention internationally.

Senge does not set out to define a learning organization as such. Rather he draws attention to the significance of learning in organizations and its consequences for organizational success. He says, for example:

> The most accurate word in Western culture to describe what happens in a learning organization is one that hasn't had much currency for the past several hundred years... The word is 'metanoia' and it means a shift of mind... To grasp the meaning of 'metanoia' is to grasp the deeper meaning of 'learning', for learning also involves a fundamental shift or movement of mind. (Senge, 1990: 13)

In Senge's view, the essence of the learning organization lies in the presence of five 'disciplines'. These are:

- personal mastery;
- mental models;
- shared vision;
- team learning;
- systems thinking.

Like Pedler *et al.*, Senge's perspective on the learning organization also draws upon numerous influences. The 'discipline' that receives most attention in the book, that of 'systems thinking', is derived from cybernetics. It is of the same family of ideas as Argyris' learning loops. Senge emphasizes other disciplines too. These include 'personal mastery', which 'goes beyond competence and skills... (and)... goes beyond spiritual unfolding or opening, although it requires spiritual growth' (1990: 141). This emphasizes a link between the personal development of employees and the capacity for organizational learning.

Applications

What impact has the thinking about learning organizations had so far on organizational practice? In an early study of the literature and practice of the learning organization, Jones and Hendry (1992) identified a number of companies that were putting these ideas into practice. Prominent among these was Shell, which took a learning approach to strategic planning. According to Jones and Hendry:

> Shell came to the conclusion that strategic planning consists of learning about the environment and people having a total view of the business in which they are employed. If more could be understood about how this learning process occurred – particularly with respect to learning in teams – ways might be found of speeding it up. A company which can accelerate its learning, according to Shell, so that it gained a year or two on its competitors, ought thereby to gain valuable commercial advantage. (Jones and Hendry, 1992: 2)

Many organizations have undoubtedly taken up the banner of learning. In Britain, for example, Rover Learning Business is a prominent example. Internationally, Motorola is well-known for its 'Motorola University'. Flesher (1995) describes a worldwide Motorola learning conference, and emphasizes the research credentials of the event.

There is much literature also on developing practices and experiments in the field. For example, Burgoyne *et al.* (1994) and Welshman *et al.* (1994), which are collections of papers from the UK Learning Company conferences, include accounts of various practical applications. O'Reilly (1995) is a collection of examples of the application of systems thinking, as popularized by Senge.

What does not yet appear to have emerged is any significant convergence of ideas or practices in the field. Whether or not such a convergence is desirable or even likely is, of course, debatable. So far we have considered themes of the learning organization as an emergent field of thinking about practical issues. We have not yet looked at the learning organization from a perspective wider than that of organizational effectiveness and tried to analyse its nature and underlying assumptions. It is to this we now turn.

A critical perspective

Authors such as Alvesson and Willmot (1992) and Thomas (1993) propose a critical perspective on ideas about management and organizations. They point out the risks of such ideas being over-influenced by the interests of managers and organizations themselves, and of failing to ask questions about the context from which the ideas have emerged.

The idea of the learning organization has been considered from such a perspective by writers such as Coopey (1995) and Dovey (1997b). For example, the notion of 'empowerment' (which Dovey remarks seems more appropriate to socialism than capitalism) is often espoused. But in practice there are highly likely to be constraints on the degree of empowerment. Genuinely empowered employees could, presumably, encroach on managerial territory. Dovey cites Jones and Hendry (1994: 156), who say that such learning 'may well create tensions within organizations which result in employees asking searching questions of a social, ethical, moral and personal kind related to the purpose of work and the nature of society'.

This political dimension of empowerment, and the potential conflicts that could be created through empowerment, receive little explicit attention in the mainstream learning-organization literature. Thus Coopey criticizes Senge and others for failing to discuss significant constraints on the concept of the learning organization. He sees them as ignoring issues such as the legal framework and 'the propensity of leaders to crave power and to lack the self-criticism sufficient to prevent that craving translating into a contempt for the rule of law (Kets de Vries, 1991) and into an unwillingness to give up power (eg Boeker, 1992)' (Coopey, 1995: 195).

Coopey argues that Argyris, Senge and others share a view that 'politicking' in organizations is undesirable. In effect, he says, they are writing from a unitarist perspective that sees the goals set by the organization as legitimate, and dissent as dysfunctional. We note for example that internal competition is often regarded as negative, but the increased competitiveness of the organization in its market-place is usually seen as virtuous.

Coopey also identifies a relatively unexamined reliance on democratic processes and wise, benevolent leaders to resolve conflict and difference. He points out the ideological potential of the idea of the learning organization, and suggests that management will exploit this to maintain their hegemony.

Given this analysis, we might ask for example whether there is evidence of learning in organizations that does challenge managerial prerogative. One would expect to find evidence of formal and informal support of learning, and evidence of genuine support for, for example, the admission of mistakes.

So this debate suggests the field of the learning organization is more an effective packaging of perhaps utopian ideas than an emergent body of sound theory. From his more pluralist perspective, Coopey suggests that learning could be both an explanatory metaphor of organizational activity and a prescription for managerial control. Ultimately he believes that:

> Those who propagate the principles of a learning organization risk opening the latest phase of a long history of metaphors which have been used manipulatively (Giddens, 1979) by managers with a long pedigree of instrumental interest in social science as a means of solving industrial problems (Pfeiffer, 1981). (Coopey, 1995: 212)

This debate also indicates something of a difference in purpose. Those advocating a critical perspective are concerned both with the quality of thinking that informs practice and with its social implications. Those such as Senge are primarily interested in developing more effective practices. But it would be simplistic to see the positions in this debate as wholly polarized. For example, Senge expresses concern with the evolution of mankind and is by no means so narrow as to focus only upon the mechanics of learning for instrumental ends. The work of the latter could be seen, in Weick's (1994) terms, as a map that facilitates action rather than one that is intended to be an accurate representation of the territory. Perhaps few authors bridge the two areas of concern, though Torbert (1991; see also Fisher and Torbert, 1995) does discuss not only forms of managerial power but also the dimension of personal development.

However, questions remain. Why is learning presented almost entirely as a good thing? There are at least two good reasons for being suspicious about this. The first is the suggestion that learning is necessarily benign and positive. As argued above, it may well be that organizations only allow for certain types of learning. Would it be perceived as a good thing, for example, for middle managers to learn to overturn senior management decisions? Or for a business to learn how to pollute the environment more effectively? The second reason is that learning then becomes seen as a panacea, a simple solution rather than a complex and often mysterious process. Argyris might well say that this was an example of a single-loop view of the phenomenon of learning itself.

Conclusion

The idea of the learning organization denotes an organization in which learning is, or is intended to be, promoted and supported, or one in which there is intentional effort to utilize organizational learning towards business goals. Organizational learning is concerned with the specific collective processes through which learning takes place.

There is no unitary theory of, or approach to, either the learning organization or organizational learning. The learning organization is a theme or frame more than a coherent system of thought. Jones and Hendry (1992) say that, in one sense, the concept is almost a dare to organizations to think and act differently. Coopey, Dovey and others regard it more as an ideological device for the maintenance of organizational power relations.

There is evidence of generally eclectic approaches. These build on the history of ideas about organizational change and development and about management learning. Some specific models and theories are associated with this broad theme, such as the ideas of Argyris on single-loop and double-loop learning.

But to what extent might Argyris and Schön's question indicate the boundaries of our concept of learning, rather than a gap in our knowledge of what happens in organizations? Developing this point, authors such as Hawkins (1994) suggest that our concept of learning is limited and outdated. He criticizes many approaches to organizational learning for their emphasis on survival and competitiveness. Included in this criticism is Reg Revans' formula about the relationship between learning and survival. Also, according to Hawkins, we tend to think of learning as an individual phenomenon, or base our concept of learning on an individual, anthropomorphic metaphor. He argues that learning is in fact a social, interpersonal and relational phenomenon as well.

The implication of this is that it could be perfectly legitimate to refer to organizations 'learning'. It is increasingly (as in Swieringa and Wierdsma, 1992, for example) common to talk of 'collective learning'. Perhaps the issue is more that our perception and language remain caught in an individualistic paradigm. It may be that the significance of organizational learning for lifelong learning lies more in the questions it raises than in the organizational practices it yields.

Chapter 14

Assessing learning

Most of the chapters in this book have been about aspects of how people learn. At first sight, assessment seems rather different. It is not about how people learn, but about whether they have learnt (and how much and what). The central question, therefore, is: how do we know that someone has learnt something?

From this point of view, the study of assessment seems relatively straightforward. What we need to do is develop techniques to discover whether learning has taken place. In fact, a large array of such techniques for assessing learning – tests, examinations and other ways of measuring performance – have been developed. Over the years they have become rather sophisticated. We discuss some of these methods in this chapter.

But the sheer sophistication and range of approaches to the assessment of learning has created its own problems. Assessment may be planned in order to discover how much learning has taken place. But in practice it has many other effects. For instance, tests play an important role in motivating learners. People's performance in examinations is used to allocate them in various ways. Depending on their exam grades, they are admitted (or not) to colleges, schools, universities, professions and jobs. We use assessments to establish our own value. For instance, we display them for all to see in our c.v.s and resumés, or in diplomas and degree certificates hanging on our office walls. People with doctorates even manage to display them in their titles.

As one very influential writer on assessment (Rowntree, 1987) has suggested, these other effects of assessment can often seem more important, or at least more urgent, than just discovering how much learning has taken place. More important, learners themselves have very often indeed seen these as the most important feature of assessment. For school students in every country, for example, assessments such as GCSEs, O-levels and A-levels are not just interesting ways of measuring how much they have learnt. They are measures which deeply influence their 'life chances': what universities and professions they will enter, how rewarding and secure their employment will be, how much they will earn, and so forth.

The unavoidable consequence of this is that the way people's learning is assessed determines to a very large extent what learning they think is important. Assessment is not therefore a 'neutral' technique for measuring the performance of learners. It has become a central feature of how learning is organized institutionally in almost every society. Assessment shapes how students, teachers and administrators think and feel about systems of education and training. Perhaps even more important, it shapes the attitudes towards learning of those who 'choose' not to undertake any formal learning after they leave school. From a 'lifelong learning' perspective, how school assessment shapes attitudes to learning and study during later life remains an important area for investigation.

The traditional approach to assessment

Longman's Dictionary of the English Language (1984), defines the verb 'to assess' as '... to determine the importance, size or value of'. The noun 'assessment' derives from this, and refers either to the process of determining importance, size or value, or to the value (size, etc) itself. The technical use of the term in education and training comes from this common-sense meaning. When used in relation to learning, therefore, assessment is about how we judge whether (and what) learning has taken (or is taking) place. (There is also a related, though less common, usage, relating to how we judge in advance a person's capacity to learn.)

In order to achieve this, assessors have built up a considerable repertoire of techniques. Underpinning these is a body of literature established over many decades. This is not the place to provide a detailed analysis of this (a useful account is provided by Rowntree, 1987), but some of the chief elements of it do call for brief discussion. Broadly speaking, the following are the key features of assessment literature as it has developed.

Formal and informal

A distinction is made between formal and informal assessment. Formal assessment is organized on some kind of official or structured basis. In contrast, we make assessments of others informally all the time. Teachers in particular make informal assessments continually of how well their students have understood what they are teaching. As a teacher, for instance, I informally assess when I ask a student whether she or he has understood a point I have just explained. Formal assessment takes place when I organize a test or examination, or when my students are entered for A-levels.

Formative and summative

A different distinction is between formative and summative assessment. Formative assessment is conducted to help plan how teaching or learning should take place, or to alter teaching or learning while it is going on. Summative assessment only tells us what has been learnt at the end of a learning or teaching process. In practice, many assessment exercises are in fact conducted partly for formative and partly for summative reasons. Nevertheless, the difference can be vital in the process of planning what we are conducting an assessment for.

Measurement

Assessment of learning involves some kind of measurement. This may be expressed in a quantitative way (as when a student gets 7 questions out of 10 correct in a test, and we award a mark of 70 per cent). Or we may attach some other system of coding our measures. Commonly used are A, B, C; but colours, the names of mathematicians, philosophers and mountains have also been used as labels in the process of measurement. One of the present authors was once awarded a 'VS' at a British university. (VS, he subsequently discovered to his chagrin, from *vix satis*, Latin for 'scarcely satisfactory'.)

Judgement

In order to measure something (eg how much a person has learnt), we must make a judgement. We must decide that a student's essay is of a B+ standard (rather than A, B or C), or that the quality of her or his progress in mathematics justifies allocation to the category Pythagoras (rather than Fibonacci or Einstein). In order to make these judgements, we must compare in some way. Assessment literature describes three main points of comparison.

- First, we can compare a learner's progress with what she or he previously knew. For instance, 'last week, Julie knew x; now she knows x + y; so she has learnt y during the past week'. This is called a self-referenced approach to assessment; it is interested only in the progress of the individual on his or her own terms, without reference to other external points of comparison.

- Second, we can compare with other people. This is very common. Many teachers and students have compared their own, or a student's, progress with other students in the class. Often this has been formalized (for example, a child's end-of-term report might state that she or he was 5th in the class in Geography, 18th in English, but 9th 'overall'). But a more rigorous approach is needed when comparing individual students' achievement not with other members of their own class, but with other students across a whole country or region. The approach typically used here is based on the fact that people's performance in examinations and tests broadly adheres to what statisticians call a 'normal distribution'. (This is the pattern sometimes described, from its shape when drawn on a graph, as a 'bell curve'.) This approach compares a person's performance with what is the norm for other people and is called a norm-referenced approach to assessment.
- Third, we can compare with some chosen criterion or criteria of performance. We can, for instance, state that in order to pass a test, a piano student must play a certain tune without error, a carpentry student must make a specific type of joint, an audio-secretary must word-process at 50 words per minute without errors. This is called a criterion-referenced approach to assessment, and has become increasingly popular over the past two decades.

Validity

Assessment literature insists that judgements must (as far as possible) be valid. This consideration is important because in relation to learning we are seldom able to measure exactly what we are really interested in. We cannot, for instance, measure precisely the whole of a student's knowledge of physics. All we can do is test in particular aspects of the subject. We can ask her or him to answer questions from memory, or conduct experiments, or write essays or discuss issues orally. All will give us some insight into what she or he knows. But each will at best provide a partial insight. (Even if it were theoretically possible to achieve a 'total snapshot' of someone's ability in a certain field, the practical difficulties of checking every aspect of knowledge and understanding would be insuperable.)

To a greater or lesser extent, therefore, every assessment instrument (test, examination, essay, etc) measures not what we would like to measure, but only a surrogate, a 'stand-in', for what we really want to measure. This leads to the concern that judgements or measures should be valid. A valid measure, put simply, is one which measures what its designers believe it measures.

Reliability

In addition to being valid, the literature stresses that assessment instruments should be reliable. This concern stems from the fact that, by and large, assessment is not applied to one person only (as with 'self-referenced' assessments), but to large groups of people, often in different places at different times. The measurements (grades, etc) are made by a large number of assessors, and most or all of them only see a small proportion of the total work. A reliable assessment instrument is one where we know that equivalent results will be given for equivalent student performance, regardless of when or where the assessment is conducted, or who conducts it.

This can, of course, be difficult to achieve. The most obvious example is in national examination (O-levels, A-levels, and GCSEs, for instance, or examinations for entry to professions such as nursing or law). How do we know that a B-grade in History A-level, for instance, means the same in terms of a student's ability in Manchester as in London (or Singapore)? Or the same in 1999, for instance, as it did in 1989, despite changes in the syllabus? There has in fact been a good deal of public debate on just this point, but on the whole these systems seem remarkable in the degree of reliability they achieve.

Contemporary issues in assessment

The above features distil the fundamental principles, terminology and concepts of the traditional literature on educational assessment. They provide the central issues which designers of assessment instruments and assessment systems are expected to bear in mind. However, the developments in thinking on lifelong learning which we have discussed in this book have had important implications for assessment. In the remainder of this chapter, we consider some of these.

Contextualized learning and assessment

Perhaps the key message of the earlier chapters of this book has been to point out that human learning is a social activity. It takes place in social situations. The context within which a person learns is fundamental. It shapes the meaning which he or she attributes to the information (or skills or attitudes) learnt. What information, skills or attitudes mean is inseparable from what we think or feel they mean.

This has a key implication for assessment. What matters is not individuals' knowledge of decontextualized bits of information, or skills, but how they apply or use this information (or skill) in real ('authentic') situations.

This approach is sometimes referred to as 'ecological' or 'performance' assessment. Ecological, because it seeks to place assessment in context; performance, because it suggests that tests should require 'some kind of active demonstration of the knowledge in question rather than a propositional account of it' (Biggs, 1996b: 26–7). The central feature is that, in a realistic setting, the learner should be asked to perform a skill or solve a problem.

This superficially resembles a behaviourist approach to assessment. Behaviourists would specify certain learning objectives, and demand that students establish that they have learnt by performing the specific behaviours described in the learning objectives. However, Biggs (1996b: 27) argues that there is a key difference. Ecological or performance assessment requires the 'qualitative assessment of applied behavioural knowledge'.

Traditionally, assessment in schools, colleges and universities has emphasized decontextualized knowledge. Until the 1980s, even examinations for professions such as law, medicine and nursing made few concessions to the real world in which knowledge would have to be applied. However, the performance or ecological approach has become more influential in recent years. It has many close parallels with the problem-based approach to learning outlined in chapter 12.

Developmental assessment and the construction of knowledge

We have argued that learning takes place in social contexts. But a second key message of this book is that learning involves an active engagement between the learner and what is being learnt. We make sense of every new experience and every new piece of information actively, in terms of our existing images of the world. As we saw in chapter 6, this is often referred to as 'constructivism'. We construct our understandings over time, connecting new pieces of information with our existing knowledge in ways which make sense to us.

One of the implications of this is that people learn cumulatively. This does not, of course, mean that they add additional bits of information to a shapeless pile of individual items of knowledge. We interpret new information and experiences in terms of our existing mental constructs. We also use this new information to review, add to and build on the constructs. Our constructs, however sophisticated, are therefore always provisional. But they are seldom utterly wrong.

Another implication is that the learner, rather than the teacher, determines what is learnt. The teacher may of course set the broad agendas, but learning only takes place if the learner engages with them. What we learn therefore depends, to a large extent, on what we already know. Anyone who has taught, particularly anyone who has taught adults, knows how important this is. If presented with new information, people try to construct an account of it which makes sense in terms of what they already know, and in terms of their existing images of the social or natural world. But they will often also resist interpretations, or knowledge, which they cannot easily reconcile with their existing constructs. In learning, the learner's role is central.

What does this mean for assessment? If we develop our knowledge based on our existing constructs, it is very difficult to distinguish 'useful' from 'useless' knowledge. This is not quite the same as saying that it is difficult to separate what is true from what is false, but there is clearly some overlap. For instance, a carpenter knows why a nail remains firmly embedded in a piece of wood, but his explanation may seem absurd to a physicist. Is the carpenter's knowledge right or wrong? If it provides a basis for improving his craftsmanship, it is clearly useful.

This points to a difficulty. The key issue in designing assessment from this perspective is not whether a learner is providing correct information. Neither is it the teacher's job to teach correct knowledge directly. The issue for the teacher is to help students to construct understandings which are 'progressively more mature and congruent with accepted thinking' (Biggs, 1996b: 25). The issue for the assessor (as for the teacher) is to judge what levels of meaning or understanding are 'reasonable', 'progressive' or 'helpful' at the appropriate stage of the learner's development.

Who should do the assessing?

Traditional views of assessment presume that the student, as the recipient of knowledge imparted by the teacher, cannot be the right person to judge whether the knowledge has been correctly learnt. Assessors need to have knowledge of the content of what is taught. By definition, this is something the learner can only be beginning to master. Assessors must also be objective. Since learners are clearly 'interested parties', we can assume they will be biased. Assessment is therefore a task to be carried out by experts. The experts may be teachers, but even teachers are often given only a modest role. (They may be big fishes in the lower-status pond of 'informal' assessment, or small fry in the higher-status assessments conducted by external examinations boards.) Stereotypically, assessment is conducted by 'objective' outsiders.

The traditional view of assessment is challenged if we think of the learner as an active agent in the learning process. There are several reasons for this. First, as we have seen, learning is regarded as constructed by the learner, rather than received from the teacher. In what sense, then, can an expert say that a learner's view is unreasonable or unhelpful? If it is helpful to the learner, can it be incorrect? Second, many learning experiences involve no teaching: they are experiential learning. Even many (planned) learning technologies now allow a large range of choice to the learner. Examples would be work-place attachments and self-access learning packages. More traditional learning examples would include creative classes (such as writing and art), or political and social education of the kind promoted by the Workers' Educational Association in Britain through most of the twentieth century. In none of these cases can we anticipate what the learner will learn. At most, learning outcomes can be only partially prescribed.

Third, in the ever-changing 'real world', we need to be able to assess our own work. Assessment is therefore not a task best delegated to a few experts. Learning to assess ourselves is in itself very worthwhile. When their training is done, the nurse must decide for himself whether his patient is fit; the solicitor must make up her own mind whether her client should sign the contract she has drafted; the mechanic must decide for himself whether the car he has repaired is now safe to drive.

For such reasons, two new approaches to assessment have emerged. Self-assessment asks the learner to assess his or her own learning. Peer-assessment asks fellow students (or fellow learners) to do so. Both clearly have the role of developing learners' own assessment skills. Advocates have argued that they have several other advantages (see, eg Biggs, 1996b; Boud, 1995).

- Students may have learnt a lot which teachers and assessors did not predict. For more sophisticated, higher cognitive types of learning in particular – 'double-loop' learning, for instance – the student is arguably a more appropriate person to decide what counts as learning than anyone else. (Biggs, 1996b)
- Even within the same course, students may learn different things, and their learning goals may well also differ. Students who are expected to set their own (perhaps differing) goals within the context of a single course, and to set for themselves their own criteria for assessing whether these goals have been achieved, may well be in the best position to decide whether their own goals have in fact been achieved. (Harris and Bell, 1986; cited by Biggs, 1996b)
- Involving the student in judging what he or she has learnt encourages a more positive attitude to learning, and increases the degree of student direction of the learning process. This has a positive impact on motivation.
- One common objection to self-assessment is made from the 'teaching' perspective. If a student's understanding ('construct') is incorrect, surely the teacher has a duty to correct it. (As Marx famously wrote, 'to leave error unrefuted is to condone intellectual immorality'.) The constructivist response would not deny the teacher's duty. Rather, it would assert that

the central learning task is not achieved by the teacher pointing out the error. The fundamental truth is that only the learner can accept that his or her construct is incorrect and reconstruct it correctly.

- Practically, there can be considerable savings in staff time, since many assessment functions are in effect delegated (Boud, 1986; from Biggs, 1996b).

Contracts, competencies and assessment

The notion that learners can play an important and active part in deciding not only what they should learn, but whether they have learnt it, is closely related to the idea of self-direction in learning. As we have seen (in chapters 9 and 10), central features of much self-directed learning literature is that the learner should be involved in establishing a 'learning contract', and should play a role (usually a large role) in judging whether this contract has been fulfilled.

Clearly formulating what should be, and judging what has been, achieved in a learning contract are assessment tasks. Boud (1995: 27–8), for example, argues that students, particularly in higher education, should become independent of their teachers. They should be expected to make decisions about what and how they learn far more than they currently are. Students using learning contracts are often asked both to determine 'criteria for assessment at the negotiation phase' and to decide when their work is 'ready to be presented for formal assessment and able to meet formal criteria' (Boud, 1995: 28).

In chapter 10 we saw that the central mechanism in Knowles' attempt to use learning contracts to support individual autonomy and control of their own learning was the idea of competence. Competence (according to Knowles) provided a mechanism which enables the learners to specify what they seek to learn in terms of clear tasks to be carried out. As we have seen, several authors (perhaps most forcefully Michael Collins) have argued that the notion of competence is inseparable from behaviourist approaches to learning. It is, from this viewpoint, a technology for control rather than for liberation or growth.

Collins' critique is implicitly contested by many who argue for the importance of self-assessment. Drawing on the work of his colleague Andrew Gonczi, Boud (1995: 59–62) develops an argument to a similar end. He suggests that in relation to education, training, and learning, the notion of competence contains a central ambiguity. It encapsulates three somewhat distinct meanings. These are:

- a task-based or behaviourist notion of competence, 'conceived in terms of the discrete behaviours associated with the completion of atomized tasks';

- a notion which focuses on 'general attributes of the practitioner' which are 'crucial to effective performance irrespective of the context in which they are applied';
- a notion which relates attributes (knowledge, attitudes, skills and values) to the context in which professionals find themselves and with which they have to deal'. (Boud, 1995: 60)

The significance of these is that, according to Boud, the first two meanings tend to separate formal knowledge from its application – having skills and being able or willing to use them in particular situations. It is the third notion which reflects the type of ability commonly called for in higher and professional education, and which encourages learners to judge how far their performance is of the required standard. As Boud points out, this still leaves unresolved the question of who sets the required standards. Competency specifications always reflect standards set by others. He tries to solve this by arguing for the importance of dialogue and a critically reflective process in setting standards. And in particular, he argues that self-assessment provides an arena in which this dialogue can happen.

More generally, Biggs (1996b) argues that when competence is related to performability, it is situated and contextualized. Although performance assessment 'recalls the behavioural objectives movement', he writes, because it is qualitatively conceived it is in fact 'the qualitative assessment of applied procedural knowledge' (Biggs, 1996b: 27). Biggs' argument relates to learning more broadly, rather than to self-assessment as such. (He does however encourage the use of self-assessment.) The importance of Biggs' argument is that, in his view, the notion of competence as performability underpins the ideas of target-oriented assessment and target-oriented curricula, such as the UK's national curriculum or Hong Kong's target-oriented curriculum.

Targets are, in effect, statements of performance which integrate teaching and assessment. Performability statements are by definition criterion-referenced (they state certain performance requirements). Target-oriented curricula are intended to provide a progressive hierarchy of performability statements. At each step or level in the hierarchy, targets are drawn up which are related to meanings or levels of understanding reasonable at certain stages of learning. The idea is that recognizable stages in the growth of competence ('key stages', in the terminology of the British national curriculum and Hong Kong's target-oriented curriculum) are also targets for teaching, learning and assessment (Biggs, 1995).

The case for a target-oriented approach is that students are given assessment tasks which enable them to see where they stand in relation to the task. They are therefore – it is argued – assessed not against each other, but against the tasks. Not only are they assessed against these targets or tasks; teaching is geared to them. The argument is that this overcomes the 'backwash' effect. Backwash is a term for one of the unintended consequence of assessment: when teachers teach and students learn not according to what the formal curriculum intends, but according to what is most likely to lead to success in assessment tasks. For students, Biggs (1995) argues, what they will be assessed on is inevitably the real target for student learning. 'The trick is to use the backwash effectively. Define quality targets and you get quality learning.'

Assessment of prior experiential learning (APEL)

Placing the notion of competence or performability at the centre of teaching and learning has another irresistible implication. Learning is no longer thought of in terms of the process by which knowledge, skills or attitudes are developed. Rather, it is seen in terms of what can be done when the learning process is complete. At the same time, emphasizing learning, rather than teaching, stresses the role of the learner rather than that of the teacher. From these, a key issue arises. If we are interested not in what a person has been taught, but in what a person knows (or can do), why should we be interested in how this knowledge, skill or attitude was attained? If a person knows something, does it matter how they came to know it?

The view that what people know or can do matters more than how they came to know it underpins the movement known as 'assessment of prior experiential learning' (APEL). Very often discussions conflate this term with the experiential learning movement as a whole, and with slogans such as 'making experience count'. This is understandable. Experiential learning is a fact; everyone learns from their experiences. The problem has always been how to make this experiential learning 'count' so far as institutions and formal education systems are concerned. The cornerstone of the attempt to make experiential learning count institutionally has been the assessment process.

Of course, in a fundamental sense the assessment of prior learning (or prior experiential learning) has been with us at least as long as assessment itself. External examination systems have long provided a method by which prior learning is assessed. For well over a century, for example, the University of London has offered examinations open to all. Typically students engage in private study and attend classes; but there has rarely been a requirement to do so. On the basis of 'mere' experience, individuals can enter such examinations and assess their state of learning.

Few advocates of experiential learning would he happy with this approach, however. They commonly argue that the syllabi imposed for such examinations and the very notion of 'unseen examinations' reflect the type of knowledge valued in traditional educational institutions. While some of this knowledge may be useful, much of it is seen as over-specialized. What matters is performability skills which students can demonstrate, rather than specific content. As a result, the experiential learning movement has tried to establish mechanisms by which individuals can be enabled not only to learn from their experience, but to realize that they have done so and demonstrate it.

The most common approach can be referred to as the 'portfolio' approach. Experiences are diverse; what matters in this is not what the experiences are, but what the individual has learnt from his or her experiences. Evans (1987; 1992) suggests a four-stage approach:

- 'Systematic reflection on experience for significant learning.' Evans (1987: 13) describes this stage as 'almost a brainstorming exercise'. Starting points may be childhood, relationships, photographs, pictures, writings, music and so forth.
- 'Identification of significant learning, expressed in precise statements, constituting claims to the possession of knowledge and skills.' The key here is to move from general identification of learning experiences, to an itemization of precisely what kinds of learning have occurred. Typically, categories of knowledge of skills can be used in this process: information handling, analysis, reading, writing skills and so on.
- 'Synthesis of evidence to support the claims made to knowledge and skills.' This involves detailed collation of evidence to support claims of learning, often in portfolio form. Guidance from tutors and counsellors is often required.
- 'Assessment for accreditation.' This begins with self-assessment, since this can influence how a student wishes to use the evidence (eg for access to education or employment). Assessment is then by staff of the educational institution, related to the knowledge and skills appropriate to the situation, and based on the evidence presented by the applicant.

Assessment, accreditation and quality assurance

Broadly speaking, education systems – the main formal systems of learning developed in most societies over the past two centuries – perform two functions: they educate and they select. They allocate people to particular social (occupational, etc) roles, and they educate (train, etc) people for these. As Biggs (1996b) points out, the relative importance of these shifts over time. In the early stages of development, the selection function is dominant. Opportunities, both occupational and for further learning, are limited. As societies and economies become more affluent, they can afford to offer opportunities for learning to more people. In post-industrial contexts, higher levels of general education within the workforce are a necessity anyhow. Learning – or at least knowledge – matters more.

Approaches to assessment which work in a highly selective educational system may not work in a system where opportunities are more diversified. Where only a very few are permitted to advance to higher levels of education, assessment can be concerned with selecting out. There may be unfairness when assessment systems favour limited social groups, but this is unlikely to lead to major social or economic inefficiencies. For society as a whole, it matters little if assessment systems discourage learning, because most people's formal learning requirements are relatively small. The few allowed into institutions of higher learning can be offered richly resourced opportunities there. These will generously compensate for any negative effects which assessment may have.

When the aim of the educational system is not so much to select the few as to ensure the many achieve a relatively high level of learning, negative 'backwash' from assessment can no longer be ignored. If assessment systems tend to demotivate students, the social and economic cost will be high. On the one hand, students will not seek to learn. On the other, more resources must be put into teaching to compensate for this lack of enthusiasm. If educational planners and administrators now see the virtues of non-traditional approaches to assessment in school systems, this – rather than idealism – is perhaps the main reason.

Nevertheless we are also seeing greater emphasis on the production of learning materials. In the chapter on distance and open learning, for instance, we noted that Peters analysed learning in terms of industrial production. In late modern society, learning is being seen as a commodity to be sold in and regulated by the market-place. With the constructivist view of knowledge, it is now very difficult to find realistic benchmarks by which to assess the outcomes of learning, except the pragmatic one that it is effective in the workplace. Now the production process needs quality management and an acceptance/accreditation of the original programme of production.

In the first chapter, we suggested thirteen major shifts that are taking place, such as from education to learning. We conclude this book by suggesting a fourteenth: from assessment to accreditation.

References

Allman, P (1984) 'Self Help Learning and its Relevance for Learning and Development in Later Life' in E Midwinter (ed.) (1984) *Mutual Aid Universities* Croom Helm, London

Alvesson, M and Willmot, H (eds) (1992) *Critical Management Studies* Sage, London

Argyris, C (1992) *On Organizational Learning* Blackwell, Oxford

Argyris, C and Schön, D (1974) *Theory in Practice: increasing professional effectiveness* Jossey Bass, San Francisco

Argyris, C and Schön, D (1978) *Organizational Learning: a theory of action perspective* Addison-Wesley, Reading, Mass.

Arlin, P (1975) 'Cognitive Development in Adulthood, a fifth stage', *Developmental Psychology*, **11**, pp602–6

Ashby, W R (1952) *Design for the Brain* Wiley, New York

Bacon, R and Eltis, W (1976) *Britain's Economic Problem: Too Few Producers* MacMillan, London

Bandura, A (1977) *Social Learning Theory* Prentice-Hall, Englewood Cliffs New Jersey

Barnett, R (1997) *Higher Education: a critical business* Open Unviersity Press, Buckingham

Barrows, H S and Tamblyn, R M (1980) *Problem Based Learning: an approach to medical education* Springer, New York

Bateson, G (1973) *Steps to an Ecology of Mind* Paladin, Granada, London

Baudrillard, J (1994) *The Illusion of the End* Polity Press, Cambridge

Baudrillard, J (1998) *The Consumer Society: myths and structures* Sage Publications, London

Bauman, Z (1987) *Legislators and Interpreters: on modernity, post-modernity and intellectuals* Polity Press, Cambridge

Bauman, Z (1991) *Modernity and Ambivalence* Polity Press, Cambridge

Bauman, Z (1992) *Intimations of Postmodernity* Routledge, London

Beck, U (1992) *Risk Society: towards a new modernity* Sage Publications, London

Belenky, M F *et al.* (1986) *Women's Ways of Knowing: the development of self, voice and mind* Basic Books, New York

Bernstein, B (1971) *Class, Codes and Control* Routledge and Kegan Paul, London

Best, S and Kellner, D (1991) *Postmodern Theory: critical interrogations* Guilford Press, New York

Biggs, J (1996a) 'Western Misperceptions of the Confucian-heritage Learning Culture', in D Watkins and J Biggs (eds) (1996) *The Chinese Learner* University of Hong Kong Comparative Education Research Centre, Hong Kong

Biggs, J (1996b) *Testing: to educate or to select?* Hong Kong Educational Publishing Co., Hong Kong

Bloom, D (ed.) (1956) *Taxonomy of Educational Objectives – Book 1, The Cognitive Domain* Longman, London

Boeker, W (1992) 'Power and Managerial Dismissal: Scapegoating at the Top', *Administrative Science Quarterly*, **37**, pp400–421

Borger, R and Seaborne, A (1966) *The Psychology of Learning* Penguin, Harmondsworth

Botkin, J, Elmandjra, M and Malitza, M (1979) *No Limits to Learning: bridging the human gap* Pergamon, Oxford

Boud, D (1986) *Implementing Student Self-Assessment* Higher Education Research and Development Society of Australia, Kensington, NSW

Boud, D (1995) *Enhancing Learning through Self Assessment* Kogan Page, London

Boud, D and Feletti, G (eds) (1991) *The Challenge of Problem Based Learning* Kogan Page, London

Boud, D, Keogh, R and Walker, D (eds) (1985) *Reflection: turning experience into learning* Kogan Page, London

Bourdieu, P and Passeron, J-C (1977) *Reproduction in Education, Society and Culture* Sage, London

Brah, A and Hoy, J (1989) 'Experiential Learning, a New Orthodoxy?', in S Weil and I McGill (eds) (1989) *Making Sense of Experiential Learning* Society for Research into Higher Education and the Open University Press, Buckingham

Brockett, R G and Hiemstra, R (1985) 'Bridging the Theory-Practice Gap in Self-Directed Learning', in S Brookfield (ed.) (1986) *Self-Directed Learning: from theory to practice* Jossey Bass, San Francisco

Brockett, R G and Hiemstra, R (1991) *Self-Direction in Adult Learning: perspectives on theory, research, and practice* Routledge, London

Brookfield, S (ed.) (1985) *Self-Directed Learning: from theory to practice* (New Directions for Continuing Education) Jossey Bass, San Francisco
Brookfield, S (1986) *Understanding and Facilitating Adult Learning* Jossey Bass, San Francisco
Brookfield, S (1987) *Developing Critical Thinkers: challenging adults to explore alternative ways of thinking and acting* Jossey Bass, San Francisco
Brookfield, S (1996) 'Helping People Learn What They Do', in D Boud and N Miller (eds) (1996) *Working with Experience* Routledge, London
Bruner, J (1968) *Toward a Theory of Instruction* W W Norton and Co, New York
Burgoyne, J, Pedler, M and Boydell, T (eds) (1994) *Towards the Learning Company* McGraw-Hill, London
Burns, T and Stalker, G M (1961) *The Management of Innovation* Tavistock, London
Casey, D (1993) *Managing Learning in Organizations* Open University Press, Buckingham
Collins, M (1991) *Adult Education as Vocation* Routledge, London
Coopey, J (1995) 'The Learning Organization, Power, Politics and Ideology', *Management Learning*, **26**, 2, pp193–213
Corden, J and Preston-Shoot, M (1987) *Contracts in Social Work* Gower, Aldershot
Department for Education and Employment (DfEE) (1996) *Lifetime Learning: a policy framework* DfEE, London
Dewey, J (1916) *Democracy and Education* Free Press, New York
Dewey, J (1938) *Experience and Education* MacMillan, New York
Dovey, K (1997a) *Reconstruction and Development in Post-Apartheid South Africa* (Unpublished PhD thesis) University of Technology, Sydney, Australia
Dovey, K (1997b) 'The Learning Organization and the Organization of Learning, Power, Transformation and the Search for Form in Learning Organizations', *Management Learning*, **28**, 3, pp331–49
Durkheim, D (1964) *The Division of Labour in Society* Free Press, New York
Engel (1991) in D Boud and G Feletti (eds) (1991) *The Challenge of Problem Based Learning* Kogan Page, London
Engestrom, Y (1987) *Learning by Expanding* Orienta-Konsultit Oy, Helsinki
Engestrom, Y (1990) *Learning, Working and Imaging* Orienta-Konsultit Oy, Helsinki
Erikson, E (1965) *Childhood and Society* Penguin, Harmondsworth
European Commission (EC) (1996) *Teaching and Learning: towards the learning society* (White Paper on Education and Training) EC, Brussels
Evans, N (1987) *Assessing Experiential Learning* Longman, London
Evans, N (1992) *Experiential Learning: assessment and accreditation* Routledge, London
Featherstone, M (1990) *Global Culture: nationalism, global culture and modernity* Sage, London

Fisher, D and Torbert, W R (1995) *Personal and Organizational Transformation* McGraw-Hill, London

Flesher, J W (1995) 'The First Motorola Worldwide Learning, Training, and Education Research Conference', *Journal of Industrial Teacher Education*, **33**, 1, pp83–5

Foucault, M (1972) *Archaeology of Knowledge* Routledge, London

Foucault, M (1986) 'What is Enlightenment?' in P Rainbow (ed.) *The Foucault Reader* Peregrine Books, Harmondsworth

Fowler, J (1981) *Stages of Faith* Harper and Row, San Francisco

Fraser, W (1995) *Learning from Experience: empowerment or incorporation?* NIACE, Leicester

Freire, P (1972) *Pedagogy of the Oppressed* Penguin, Harmondsworth

Further Education Funding Council (FEFC) (1997) *Learning Works: widening participation in further education* (The Kennedy report) FEFC, Coventry

Gardner, H (1989) *To Open Minds* Basic Books, New York

Garratt, R (1987) *The Learning Organization* Fontana/Collins, London

Giddens, A (1979) *Central Problems in Social Theory* Macmillan, London

Giddens, A (1993) *The Consequences of Modernity* Polity Press, Cambridge

Giddens, A (ed.) (1992) *Global Politic: globalization and the nation state* Polity Press, Cambridge

Gilligan, C (1982) *In a Different Voice: psychological theory and women's development* Harvard University Press, Cambridge, Mass.

Goleman, D (1995) *Emotional Intelligence* Bloomsbury, London

Griffin, C (1983) *Curriculum Theory in Adult and Lifelong Education* Croom Helm, London

Griffin, C (1987) *Adult Education as Social Policy* Croom Helm, London

Habermas, J (1972) *Knowledge and Human Interests* Heinemann, London

Habermas, J (1984) *The Theory of Communicative Action*, Volume 1, Polity Press, Cambridge

Habermas, J (1992) *The Philosophical Discourse of Modernity* Polity Press, Cambridge

Hales, C (1993) *Managing Through Organisation* Routledge, London

Handy, C (1989) *The Age of Unreason* Business Books Ltd (Century Hutchinson), London

Harris, D and Bell, C (1986) *Evaluating and Assessing for Learning* Kogan Page, London

Hau, K T and Salili, F (1991) 'Structure and Semantic Differential Placement of Specific Causes: academic causal attributions by Chinese students in Hong Kong', *International Journal of Psychology*, **26**, 2, pp175–93

Hawkins, P (1991) 'The Spiritual Dimension of the Learning Organization', *Management Education and Development*, **22**, 3, pp172–87

Hawkins, P (1994) 'The Changing View of Learning', in J Burgoyne, M Pedler and T Boydell (eds) (1994) *Towards the Learning Company* McGraw-Hill, London

Heller, A (1984) *Everyday Knowledge* Routledge and Kegan Paul, London
Henfield, V J and Waldron, R (1988) 'The Use of Competency Statements to Facilitate Individualised Learning', *Nurse Education Today* **8**, pp205–211
Hirst, P Q (1996) *Globalization in Question* Polity Press, Cambridge
Holford, J (1994) *Union Education in Britain* Nottingham University, Nottingham
Holmberg, B (1995 2nd edn) *Theory and Practice of Distance Education* Routledge, London
Hooper, F (1960 2nd edn; 1st edn 1948) *Management Survey* Penguin, Harmondsworth
Houle, C O (1961) *The Inquiring Mind* University of Wisconsin Press, Madison
Houle, C O (1972) *The Design of Education* Jossey Bass, San Francisco
Houle, C O (1984) *Patterns of Learning* Jossey Bass, San Francisco
Illich, I (1971) *Deschooling Society* Calder and Boyars, London
Jarvis, P (1972) *Religious Socialisation in the Junior School* (Unpublished M Soc Sc thesis) University of Birmingham, Birmingham
Jarvis, P (1985) *The Sociology of Adult and Continuing Education* Croom Helm, London
Jarvis, P (1987) *Adult Learning in the Social Context* Croom Helm, London
Jarvis, P (1992) *Paradoxes of Learning* Jossey Bass, San Francisco
Jarvis, P (1997) *Ethics and Education for Adults in a Late Modern Society* NIACE, Leicester
Jarvis, P (1998) *From Practice to Theory* Jossey Bass, San Francisco
Jones, A M and Hendry, C (1992) *The Learning Organization: A Review of Literature and of Practice* Centre for Corporate Strategy and Change, Warwick Business School, University of Warwick
Jones, A M and Hendry, C (1994) 'The Learning Organization, Adult Learning and Organizational Transformation', *British Journal of Management*, **5**, pp153–62
Kant, I (1993 edn cited; 1st edn 1788) *Critique of Pure Reason* J M Dent, London
Keegan, D (1990 2nd edn) *Foundations of Distance Education* Routledge, London
Keegan, D (ed.) (1993) *Theoretical Principles of Distance Education* Routledge, London
Kelly, T (1970 2nd edn) *A History of Adult Education in Great Britain* Liverpool University Press, Liverpool
Kets de Vries, M (1991) 'Whatever Happened to the Philosopher King? The Leader's Addiction to Power', *Journal of Management Studies*, **28**, **4**, pp339–51
Kett, J F (1994) *The Pursuit of Knowledge Under Difficulties* Stanford University Press, Stanford
Kidd, R (1973 revised edn) *How Adults Learn* Association Press, Chicago

Knowles, M (1970) *The Modern Practice of Adult Education: Andragogy vs Pedagogy* Association Press, New York
Knowles, M (1975) *Self-Directed Learning: a guide for learners and teachers* Association Press, New York
Knowles, M (1980 2nd edn) *The Modern Practice of Adult Education* Association Press, Chicago
Knowles, M (1986) *Using Learning Contracts* Jossey Bass, San Francisco
Kohlberg, L (1986) *The Philosophy of Moral Development* Harper and Row, San Francisco
Kolb, D (1984) *Experiential Learning* Prentice Hall, Englewood Cliffs, New Jersey
Kolb, D and Fry, R (1975) 'Toward an Applied Theory of Experiental Learning', in C L Cooper (ed.)(1975) *Theories of Group Processes* John Wiley and Sons, London
Lash, S *et al.* (eds) (1996) *Risk, Environment and Modernity: towards a new ecology* Sage Publications, London
Lave, J and Wenger, E (1991) *Situated Learning* Cambridge University Press, Cambridge
Lawton, D (1973) *Social Change, Educational Theory and Curriculum Planning* Hodder and Stoughton, London
Lessem, R (1993) *Business as a Learning Community: applying global concepts to organizational learning* McGraw-Hill, London
Levinson, D (1978) *The Seasons of a Man's Life* Knopf, New York
Lewin, K (1951) *Field Theory in the Social Sciences* Harper and Row, New York
Long, H *et al.* (1992) *Self-Directed Learning: Application and Research* Oklahoma Research Center for Continuing Professional and Higher Education of the University of Oklahoma
Longman's Dictionary of the English Language (1984) Longman, Harlow
Lyotard, J-F (1974) *The Post-Modern Condition* Manchester University Press, Manchester
Lyotard, J-F (1984) *The Postmodern Condition: a report on knowledge* University of Minnesota Press, Minneapolis
Marsick, V (ed.) (1987) *Learning in the Workplace* Croom Helm, London
Marsick, V J and Watkins, K (1990) *Informal and Incidental Learning in the Workplace* Routledge, London and New York
Maslow, A (1968 2nd edn) *Towards a Psychology of Being* Van Nostrand, New York
McAllister, M (1996) 'Learning contracts, an Australian experience', *Nurse Education Today*, **16**, 199-205
Mead, G H (1934) *Mind, Self, and Society: from the standpoint of a social behaviorist* University of Chicago Press, Chicago
Mead, G H (1977) *George Herbert Mead on Social Psychology, selected papers* (ed. A Strauss) University of Chicago Press, Chicago

Merton, R (1968) *Social Theory and Social Structure* Free Press, New York

Mezirow, J (1991) *Transformative Dimensions of Adult Learning* Jossey Bass, San Francisco

Mezirow, J *et al.* (1990) *Fostering Critical Reflection in Adulthood* Jossey Bass, San Francisco

Miller, N and Boud, D (1996) 'Animating Learning from Experience', in D Boud and N Miller (eds) (1996) *Working with Experience* Routledge, London

Miller, D L (1973) *George Herbert Mead: self, language and the world* University of Texas Press, Austin

Ministry of Reconstruction, Cmd 321 (1919) *Ministry of Reconstruction, Adult Education Committee: Final Report* HMSO, London

Mintzberg, H (1979) *The Structuring of Organizations* Prentice-Hall, Englewood Cliffs, New Jersey

Moore, M (1980) 'Independent Study', in R D Boyd *et al.* (1980) *Redefining the Discipline of Adult Education* Jossey-Bass, San Francisco

Moore, M (1993) 'Three Types of Interaction', in K Harry, M John and D Keegan (eds) (1993) *Distance Education: new perspectives* Routledge, London

Morgan, G (1997 2nd edn) *Images of Organization* Sage, London

Moshman, D (1979) 'To Really Get Ahead, Get a Metatheory', in D Kuhn (ed.) (1979) *Intellectual Development Beyond Childhood* Jossey Bass, San Francisco

National Advisory Group for Continuing Education and Lifelong Learning (NAGCELL) (1997) *Learning for the Twenty-first Century* (The Fryer Report) NAGCELL, London

National Committee of Inquiry into Higher Education (NCIHE) (1997) *Higher Education in the Learning Society: report of the National Committee* (The Dearing Report) NCIHE, London

National Institute of Adult and Continuing Education (NIACE) (1996) *Through the Joy of Learning: diary of 1,000 adult learners* (eds P Coare and A Thomson) NIACE, Leicester

National Institute of Adult and Continuing Education (NIACE) (1997) *Lifelong Learning in England and Wales* NIACE, Leicester

Neugarten, B (1977) 'Adult Personality: Towards a Psychology of the Life-Cycle', in P Allman and D Jaffe (eds) (1977) *Readings in Adult Psychology* Harper, New York

O'Reilly, K W (ed.) (1995) *Managing the Rapids: stories from the forefront of the learning organization* Pegasus Communications Ltd, Cambridge, Mass.

Oakeshott, M (1933) *Experience and its Modes* Cambridge University Press, Cambridge

OECD (1973) *Recurrent Education: a strategy for lifelong learning* OECD, Paris

Ormrod, J (1995 2nd edn) *Human Learning* Merrill, Englewood Cliffs, NJ

Parsons, T (1951) *The Social System* Routledge and Kegan Paul, London

Paul, R H (1993) 'Open Universities: the test of all models', in K Harry, M John and D Keegan (eds) (1993) *Distance Education: new perspectives* Routledge, London

Pedler, M, Boydell, T and Burgoyne, J (1989) 'Towards the Learning Company', *Management Education and Development*, **20**, 1, pp1–8

Pedler, M, Boydell, T and Burgoyne, J (1991) *The Learning Company* McGraw-Hill, London

Peters, O (1993) 'Understanding Distance Education', in K Harry, M John and D Keegan (eds) (1993) *Distance Education: new perspectives* Routledge, London

Peters, R (1966) *Ethics and Education* George Allen and Unwin, London

Peters, R (1977) *Education and the Education of Teachers* Routledge and Kegan Paul, London

Pfeiffer, J (1981) *Power in Organization* Ballinger, Cambridge, Mass.

Piaget, J (1929) *The Child's Conception of the World* Routledge and Kegan Paul, London

Pratt, J (1985) 'Juvenile Justice, Social Work and Social Control', *British Journal of Social Work*, **15**, pp1–24

Reich, R (1991) *The Work of Nations* Simon and Schuster, London

Revans, R (1980) *Action Learning* Blond and Biggs, London

Revans, R (1983) 'Action Learning: its origins and nature', in M Pedler (ed.) (1983) *Action Learning in Practice* Gower, Aldershot

Richardson, M (1988) 'Innovating Andragogy in a Basic Nursing Course: an evaluation of the sef directed independent study contract with basic nursing students', *Nurse Education Today*, **8**, pp315–24

Riegel, K (1973) 'Dialectical Operations: the final period of cognitive development', in *Human Development*, **16**, 3, pp346–70

Robertson, R (1992) *Globalization: social theory and global culture* Sage Publications, London

Rodger, J (1991) 'Discourse Analysis and Social Relationships in Social Work', *British Journal of Social Work*, **21**, pp63–79

Rojek, C and Collins, S A (1987) 'Contract or Con-trick?', *British Journal of Social Work*, **17**, pp199–211

Roth, G L and Niemi, J (1996) 'Information Technology Systems and the Learning Organization', *International Journal of Lifelong Education*, **15**, 3, pp202–15

Rowntree, D (1987 2nd edn) *Assessing Students: how shall we know them?* Kogan Page, London,

Rumble, G (1995) 'Labour Market Theories and Distance Education', *Open Learning* **10**, 1–3

Rumble, G and Harry, K (eds)(1982) *The Distance Teaching Universities* Croom Helm, London

Salili, F (1996) 'Accepting Personal Responsibility for Learning' in D A Watkins, and J B Biggs (eds) (1996) *The Chinese Learner: cultural, psychological and contextual influences* University of Hong Kong Comparative Education Research Centre, Hong Kong

Schön, D (1983) *The Reflective Practitioner* Basic Books, New York

Schön, D (1987) *Educating the Reflective Practitioner* Jossey Bass, San Francisco

Senge, P (1990) *The Fifth Discipline* Century Business, Random Century, London

Social Trends, 27 (1997) HMSO, London

Stata, R (1994) 'Organizational Learning – The Key to Management Innovation', in W L French, C H Bell and R A Zawacki (eds) (1994 4th edn) *Organization Development and Transfomation* Irwin, Burr Ridge, Illinois

Stehr, R (1994) *Knowledge Society* Sage, London

Stenhouse, L (1975) *An Introduction to Curriculum Research and Development* Heinemann, London

Stephenson, J and Laycock, M (eds) (1993) *Using Learning Contracts in Higher Education* Kogan Page, London

Stikkers, K (1980) *Problems of a Sociology of Knowledge – Max Scheler* Routledge and Kegan Paul, London

Swieringa, J and Wierdsma, A (1992) *Becoming a Learning Organization: beyond the learning curve* Addison-Wesley, Wokingham

Tang, C (1996) 'Collaborative learning: the latest dimension in Chinese students' learning' in D A Watkins and J B Biggs, (eds) (1996) *The Chinese Learner: cultural, psychological and contextual influences* University of Hong Kong Comparative Education Research Centre, Hong Kong

Thomas, A B (1993) *Controversies in Management* Routledge, London

Toffler, A (1970) *Future Shock* Bantam Books, New York

Torbert, W (1991) *The Power of Balance* Sage, Newbury Park, California

Tough, A (1979 2nd edn) *The Adult's Learning Projects* Ontario Institute for Studies in Education, Toronto

Tough, A (1982) *Intentional Changes: a fresh approach to helping people change* Follett Publishing Co., Chicago

Tough, A (1993) 'Self-Planned Learning and Major Personal Change', in R Edwards *et al.* (eds) (1993) *Adult Learners, Education and Training: a reader* Routledge and Open University Press, London

UNESCO (1996) *Learning: the treasure within* by J Delors (Report by the International Commission for the Twenty-first Century) UNESCO/HMSO, London

Usher, R and Edwards, R (1994) *Postmodernism and Education* Routledge, London

Vygotsky, L (1978) *Mind in Society* Harvard University Press, Cambridge, Mass.

Vygotsky, L (1986) *Thought and Language* (revised and edited by A Kozulin) MIT, Cambridge, Mass.

Waters, M (1995) *Globalization* Sage Publications, London

Watkins, D A and Biggs, J B (eds) (1996) *The Chinese Learner: cultural, psychological and contextual influences* University of Hong Kong Comparative Education Research Centre, Hong Kong

Watkins, K and Marsick, V (1993) *Sculpting the Learning Organization* Jossey Bass, San Francisco

Weick, K (1994) 'Cartographic Myths in Organisations', in H Tsoukas (ed.) (1994) *New Thinking in Organizational Behaviour* Butterworth-Heinemann, Oxford

Weil, S and McGill, I (eds) (1989) *Making Sense of Experiential Learning* Society for Research into Higher Education and the Open University Press, Buckingham

Welshman *et al.* (eds) (1994) *Learning Company Conference 1994: collected papers* The Learning Company Project, Sheffield

Workers' Educational Association (1953) *Trade Union Education* WEA, London

Name Index

Subject Index